THE OFFICIAL
POLITICALLY INCORRECT
HANDBOOK

D0808777

Nine other politically incorrect books by the same authors

- The Complete Revenge Kit
- How to Be a Complete Bastard (with Adrian Edmondson)
- How to Be a Complete Bitch (with Pamela Stephenson)
- The Book of Revelations
- The Naughty 90s
- The Return of the Complete Revenge Kit
- How to Be a Superhero
- The Book of Stupid Lists
- How to Be a Real Man (with Julian Clary)

THE OFFICIAL POLITICALLY INCORRECT HANDBOOK

Mike Lepine
and Mark Leigh

Virgin

DEDICATION

For Raglan, the golden retriever. Born 9 July 1990 on a Welsh puppy farm, put to sleep due to 'rage syndrome' 1 August 1991, aged one year three weeks. Rest in peace, Rags. We love you.

Mike and Philippa.

Don't buy animals from pet shops.

First published in Great Britain in 1993 by
Virgin Books
an imprint of Virgin Publishing Ltd
332 Ladbroke Grove
London W10 5AH

A catalogue record for this book is available from the British Library.

ISBN 0 86369 748 8

Phototypeset by Intype Ltd, London

Printed and bound in Great Britain by
Cox & Wyman, Reading, Berks

Politically Incorrect people who have helped us with this book

Peter Bennett Speck, Stephen Choopani, Gary Fairhead, Chris Fordwoh, Paul Forty, Philippa Hatton, Sally Holloway, Neville Landau, Debbie Leigh, Judy Martin, Kate Ogles, Julie Smith.

Many a true word is
spoken in jest

DISCLAIMER

The views expressed by the authors herein are not necessarily those of Virgin Publishing or its employees and agents, including their MD (and he's got some strange opinions, if truth be known). In fact if we'd known what they were going to say we might have been able to stop them. They said it was going to be satirical instead of abusive — and we fell for it. Anyway, we apologise if anyone is offended by any of the contents and would like to reassure you that neither writer was paid very much for this, if that's any consolation.

ABATTOIRS — some nice names for these establishments to help appease animal lovers

- Golden Slumbers Animal Lodge
- Serenity Glades Home for Elderly Quadrupeds
- Tranquillity Bay Bovine Depository
- The Farmer's Friends Chapel of Rest
- Twilight Hours Sheep Sanctuary
- The Last Round-up
- The Beasts of Burden Hall of Peace

ABORIGINES — good fantasies to have during 'dream time'

- Playing a blistering three-minute didgeridoo solo in front of 100,000 screaming chicks in the Melbourne Astrodome
- Spending two days (and nights) locked in a suite at the Brisbane Hilton with the Barbi Twins and a tub of Vegemite
- Being 'Mad Max'
- Playing 'lead wobble board' with INXS
- Having a luxury four-door Lada to live in rather than an old rusty wreck

1

- Waking up and finding out that all the white men have fucked off back to Europe

ADULT EDUCATION — why it should be discontinued

- It will serve people right for messing around when they were at school
- Men wearing short trousers and a cap look silly
- If these people can't read, how will they understand the syllabus (or even know what day the term starts?)
- Gobbing at the blackboard no longer holds the appeal it once did
- Once you reach 30 you resent people giving you nicknames like 'stinker', 'fatso' or 'shortarse'
- Neither do you enjoy being called 'menopausey', 'baldy' or 'alki'
- When it comes to the open evening, most of the parents would be dead
- School sports days usually result in a series of massive cardiac arrests

AFFAIRS — why they're a good idea

- You can sneak away when you're bored without a messy (and expensive) legal battle
- The marriage vows don't say 'Do you promise not to have a sordid, shabby affair?'
- If your marriage does break up you won't have to go far to find a new partner
- Trying to think of all those excuses for working late really keeps you on your toes
- They enable you to have more than one partner without having to become a Mormon or join another whacko religious cult
- It's a very French thing to do — and we're always being encouraged to become more European . . .

AGONY AUNTS — answers we'd love to see them give

- 'Don't ask stupid questions'
- 'Will you piss off, lovey? Will you, will you do that for me, lovey? Will you piss off?'
- 'It's all your own fault'
- 'I get letters like yours every day. What's wrong with you people? Are you all stupid or something?'
- 'Wait until he's asleep and then snip off his bollocks'
- 'It's a sin against God and you'll burn in hell for all eternity, you trollop!'
- 'I don't care'
- 'Sorry, your situation is hopeless, you inadequate, socially repugnant little tic'
- 'Take 200 paracetamol and put yourself out of your misery'
- 'Stay with whichever one of them has the biggest cock'

ALCOHOLISM — why it's a good thing

- You don't know that you are one
- Everyone in the world is your best mate
- You don't remember a thing about walking naked down the high street, trying to have sex with a traffic cone which you thought was Kim Basinger
- It prevents you having sex (useful if you're not in the mood anyway)
- It helps to bring the rest of your family together
- By the time you realise what's happened to you, you don't have enough living brain cells left to care
- Cirrhosis of the liver lets you get your money's worth out of the NHS in one fell swoop

- You can hang out with celebrities at special clinics
- If all else fails, you can always find secure employment as a Spanish air traffic controller

ALTERNATIVE FUELS — some solidly politically incorrect ideas

- Ivory
- Blubber
- The clergy
- Greenpeace leaflets
- Monkey brains
- Anything that creates plenty of carbon dioxide when it's burnt
- Leopard pelts
- Poor people
- Mahogany
- Shampoo that's only been tested on animals

THE AMAZON RAIN FOREST — why it should be turned into the world's largest amusement park

- Brazil could use the foreign currency that tourists bring in
- All the unemployed natives could be gainfully employed going around dressed as famous cartoon characters
- For traditionalists, there could be a special 'native village' set up to show what life in the rain forest used to be like — populated by animatronic life-like dummies
- There's plenty of spare timber around to build the attractions and rides
- Being in a Third World country, the rides don't have to be as safe as they do in the developed world, making them cheap and easy to maintain
- Big-breasted women could dress up as the fabled Amazons to keep the dads entertained

- Some elements of native culture could be maintained — like blowpipe-shooting stalls and decorated toffee apples made to look like shrunken heads
- It would be better than EuroDisney

AMBULANCE SERVICE, TODAY'S — things that are quicker

- An unambitious tortoise
- A snail dragging a ball and chain
- A slug going backwards
- Being rushed to hospital by steamroller
- Mike Morris's wits
- The third day's play in the Test at Lords
- Tax refunds
- British Rail

AMERICA — why it's neither the home of the free nor the brave

- Instead of being free, medicine costs an absolute fortune — and the welfare state barely exists
- The brave is stuck on some shithole reservation in the Dakota Badlands

AMERICA — why it must never elect a female president

- It sounds stupid to say 'Hail to the Chiefess'
- It sounds equally stupid to say 'Good afternoon, Mrs President'
- If she has particularly bad PMT or a tiff with her boyfriend one morning, she'll press the button
- She'll keep having to go to the bathroom during vital strategic arms limitation talks
- She might fall truly, madly, deeply in love with a brutal yet handsome Middle Eastern dictator, forging a very odd alliance

- People might say 'Hey, look at the tits on that President!'
- If Congress blocks one of her proposals, she might burst into tears
- She might refuse to fly on a vital diplomatic mission because she's waiting for a phone call from her boyfriend
- One day she could be called upon in the middle of the night to make a split-second decision — and she'll insist on 'putting her face on' first

AMERICAN DECLARATION OF INDEPENDENCE — why not all men are created equal

- Some are taller
- Some resemble Mel Gibson — others Mel Smith
- Some have rich parents
- Some are born with a $200-a-day cocaine habit
- Some are planned . . .
- Some are women
- Some feel they should have been born women (but were cheated by an accident of birth)
- Some are white
- Some aren't . . .

THE AMERICAN SOUTH — why the south *will* rise again

- Scum always rises to the surface

ANIMAL SLAUGHTERING — some quite inhumane methods of killing cows

- Herd them through a minefield
- Hit them on the head with a shovel yelling, 'Die, cow, die!'
- Strangle them with a silk scarf
- Explode a small Semtex charge up their rectum
- Publicly lynch them in front of an angry mob

- Tie them to a railway track
- Push them out of an Inter City 125 and claim the door was faulty
- Push them out of a twelfth-storey window (and make it look like an accident)
- Fire a metal bolt into their brains and string them up on a conveyor belt to be chain-sawed, often while they're still alive (Whoops! That's how it's really done)

ANIMAL SLAUGHTERING — one method which is *never* used to kill cows

- Kindness

ANIMAL TESTING — why it's vital

- What human in their right mind would want hairspray sprayed continuously in their eyes, or volunteer for burns testing?
- If we didn't have shampoo, we'd all look like Bob Geldof
- If they didn't develop new and better cosmetics women wouldn't have anything to blow their housekeeping money on
- If a clothing manufacturer had big plans to make underwear which exploded with the force of Krakatoa, it's better that 300 chimpanzees are spread across the Home Counties than you being scraped off C&A's dressing rooms
- With everyone giving up smoking these days it's only the beagles that keep Rothmans in business
- If we hadn't used kittens to find out what the inside of a microwave feels like, innocent people might be putting their heads in them today
- Without it, no member of the public would ever

know what a monkey looks like with its brain
exposed

ANOREXIA NERVOSA — why it's a brilliant illness to have

- You can fit into a size 4 without straining the seams
- You can dash out in the rain without getting wet
- You can dress in yellow, wear a pointed hat and go to a fancy dress party as an HB pencil
- Because your clothes are that much smaller you can take more of them away on holiday with you
- You can save money by buying children's clothes
- It makes your Nissan Micra feel like a limo
- You can participate in a three-in-a-bed romp — in a single bed!
- You don't have the hassle of having to buy bras — or tampons
- You have a figure most girls would die for

ANTARCTICA — why it's good to exploit its mineral deposits

- You can make a load of money
- Africa's mineral deposits are almost exhausted and the West needs a fresh continent to ponce off
- Hardly anyone will complain about the drilling noise
- If they do, it's likely to be the penguins — and you can always buy them off with fish
- After a hard day's exploitation you can unwind with some relaxing ice-skating or snowball fights with rival base camps
- It gives you a chance to drive a Sno-Cat (and they're brilliant!)
- You'll never, ever get lost (everywhere is 'South')

- What else is Antarctica good for?

ARGENTINIAN PRISONERS OF WAR — excuses 3 Para should have given for shooting them

- 'I wanted their ears for my necklace'
- 'The Argentinian for "I surrender" sounds very similar to "Please tie my hands behind my back, blindfold me, line me up in front of a trench and shoot me in the head" '
- 'War is hell!'
- ' "Prisoners of war"? I thought they were "Prisoners of conscience" and was just doing what the Argentinian government normally does . . .'
- 'There's nothing to do in the Falklands and I was bored'
- 'I did it for Simon Weston'
- 'He went to blow his nose and I thought he was going for a Cruise missile in his pocket, sir'
- 'I was feeling left out 'cos I hadn't killed anyone in combat, like all my mates'
- 'I've always wanted to appear on a *World in Action* special'
- 'I was only following orders'

ARMS — why it was a good idea to sell them to Iraq

- If we didn't, they'd only buy them from somewhere else
- It was a good way to learn about Iraq's military build-up
- Their credit was good
- They offered a better price than Iran
- It was better than selling them to Libya
- Selling direct and cutting out the middle men (i.e. international arms dealers) meant that prices could be made more attractive

- They were safer in the hands of Iraqis than the Americans who managed to kill more of our boys than the enemy did
- Most of the weapons we produce are duds so our boys were completely safe storming the enemy lines

AROMATHERAPY — a guide to the effects of different fragrances

- Basil — none
- Clary sage — none
- Hyssop — none
- Jasmine — none
- Marjoram — none
- Orange flower absolute — none
- Rosemary — none
- Sandalwood — none
- Verbena — none
- Ylang-Ylang — none

ART-HOUSE FILMS — why they're crap

- They're all in French and you have to read subtitles
- The subtitles invariably get in the way of the girl's pubes
- They also get in the way of the man's willie — if you're so inclined
- Very few of the characters ever get to use chainsaws or rocket launchers on each other
- Some of them are in black and white for some reason
- Art-house movies don't have proper plots; they just feature characters wandering around, chain-smoking Gauloises and saying how all life is suffering for what seems like nine hours
- Middle-class pseudo-intellectual liberal gits like

10

them — and then go around talking about
'Francis Truffle'
- If they were any good, they wouldn't be art-house films

AUSTRALIA — the 10 most empty buildings on the continent (or the earth, for that matter)

- The Melbourne Public Library
- The Sydney Opera House
- The Ballet de Perth
- The Alice Springs Art Gallery
- The home of the Adelaide Symphony Orchestra
- The Art-house Cineplex, Woolamagong
- The Indoor Canberra Flower Festival
- The National Theatre, Brisbane
- Books R Us, Sydney
- The Museum of Australian Culture, Canberra

THE AZTECS — why they really asked for it

- They thought the invading Spaniards were gods (and if anyone who worships the Spanish doesn't deserve being wiped off the face of this earth, then who does?)
- They went around boasting of a city made of solid gold called 'Eldorado'. If they'd any sense whatsoever they'd have called it something deliberately off-putting like 'El Black Death', 'El Cesspito', 'El Turdos Grande' or 'Basildon'
- They hadn't even invented the wheel by the sixteenth century (how hard is it to invent the wheel? All you have to do is cut a bit off the end of a log)
- They all had silly names like 'Quetzalcoatl', 'Tezcatlipoca' and 'Xochiquetzal' which are great for Scrabble but nothing else
- This also hindered their development of poetry (in fact, they gave up in the eleventh century

11

after getting stuck on 'There was a young man called Yacacoliuhqui . . .')

- They gave their settlements equally stupid names (would you want to live somewhere called 'Lake Titicaca'?)
- One of their gods, Xolotl, was the patron of ball games
- They believed that drilling a hole in your head would release evil spirits rather than killing you instantly
- They believed that human sacrifice would make their race prosper . . .

BABIES — 10 politically incorrect names to lumber them with

- Adolf
- Benito
- Maggie
- Saddam
- Idi
- Genghis
- Jeremy-Mengele
- Tojo
- Oswald Mosley Junior
- Martin Luther Twat

BABY SEAL CULLING — why it's a good idea

- It gives the French Canadians something to do
- You have to get them before they get you
- Anything that cute deserves it
- They make great fur coats (if they culled the old seals your fur coat would look manky and bald)
- It's good practice for the baseball season
- It keeps car sticker manufacturers in work
- It saves the seals suffering a lingering death when the latest super-tanker disaster happens
- They make a very satisfying crunchy sound when you hit them
- You go home at the end of the day with a truly Hemingway-esque experience

BALD MEN — why they're *not* sexy

- You can't run your fingers through their hair
- Kissing their heads is like kissing a buttock
- They refuse to hang upside down from a chandelier in case their wig falls off
- When they get all hot and sweaty the adhesive holding their wig on starts to melt and drip into your face
- It's like making love to Duncan Goodhew, Danny DeVito or that orange git in the Tango commercial (yuk!)
- They're always pestering you to let them try the Pill just so they can see if it has any side-effects — like making their hair grow
- When you suggest 'giving head' they get all self-conscious

BALD WOMEN — why they're not sexy either

- They probably have some dreaded lurgy
- They may well have shaved their head as a last resort against nit-infestation
- It would be like sleeping with Sinéad O'Connor — no thank you
- You can't shake this nagging doubt that they *just might* be a man in drag
- You could reasonably expect them to be 'not all there'
- They might have a skinhead boyfriend
- Sigourney Weaver looked like shit in *Aliens 3*
- People stare at you when you go out in the street together and make all kinds of assumptions
- Girlfriends should have proper nicknames, like 'cutey' and 'sweetie' and 'Miss Piggy' — not 'Slaphead' or 'Bald Bird'

BAIL — why it should be abolished

- Because once you let the scrotes out of custody, they'll just commit the same crime again
- And again
- And again
- And again
- And again
- And again
- And again
- And again
- And again
- And again

BATTERY FARM — how to set up your own intensive farming operation for fun and profit!

- Allow four inches of cage width per bird, with four or five birds to a cage
- As a rough idea, the chicken should spend its entire life in an area just slightly bigger than this page
- Cages should be stacked three or four levels high in windowless buildings
- You may find some of your stock going a bit loopy and pecking themselves; in this case de-beak them. This is painful, roughly equivalent to having your fingernails pulled off, but widely accepted in battery farming circles
- As soon as your egg-laying chickens approach the age of two, their egg yield starts to decrease, so kill them
- Replace them with young females. Useless one-day-old male chicks may be killed by crushing them together into a pulp using a special mill capable of squashing 500 chicks a minute
- This, however, requires an expensive piece of kit. If you resent investing in this, simply put all the

15

chicks into a sealed box and wait for them to starve or suffocate
- The eggs you'll produce by battery farming are inferior and contain 40 per cent less vitamin B12 and 30 per cent less folic acid than free-range eggs — but it's all right; no one knows that
- They *do* know about salmonella, but they've largely forgotten

BATTERY HEN FARMING — why it should be encouraged

- It prevents the hens suffering from agoraphobia
- It saves them having to decide what they should do today
- It prevents them getting eaten by foxes
- It gives them an insight into how the Lebanese hostages must have felt
- It keeps the cost of eggs down
- The farmers know where their hens are at any given time

BEAGLES — why they like to smoke cigarettes

- It makes them feel confident
- They can save up the coupons to buy that dartboard they've always wanted
- They can use cigarette holders and look all suave and sophisticated
- It impresses the girl beagles
- It makes them look older so they can get into '18' movies
- It gives them something to do while they're clamped in their laboratory cages
- It's better than having shampoo squirted in their eyes

BEGGARS — good things to give them apart from money

- A wide berth
- The finger
- Merry hell
- The cold shoulder
- Lip
- No mercy
- A piece of your mind
- Short shrift
- The flu
- Sweet F.A.

BENETTON — some suggestions for future posters

- A slaughtered cow wearing a Walkman
- Three partisans being hanged with piano wire
- A cat that's just been run over by a van
- Jesus on the cross wearing a bra
- Two amputees in a hammer fight
- Someone who's just jumped to their death from a twelve-storey window
- Some brightly coloured knitwear on an attractive model — for a real shocker!

BERLIN WALL — why they should rebuild it

- Rebuilding it will provide employment for all those East Germans who streamed into the West but who still haven't found jobs
- Those without jobs as builders can work as searchlight operators, border guards and machine-gunners
- It will be a tourist attraction once again, bringing in welcome foreign currency
- With 128 miles of reinforced concrete it would be a grand symbol of German construction and engineering skills

- It would be good news for the manufacturers of razor wire
- It would teach the East Germans never to take anything for granted
- It's a good place to paint anti-fascist slogans
- You could use it as a massive squash court
- It's a convenient way for the Germans to keep immigrants out

BESTIALITY — why it should be legalised immediately

- You can't catch social diseases from animals — so what better form of 'safe sex' could there be?
- Legalisation would save filling our jails up with loonies whose only crime was to fancy a bit of spaniel
- Zoos could make the money they need to survive by turning into giant brothels
- You don't know what sex really is until you've been with an emperor penguin
- The Welsh would be able to practise their national pastime without fear of moral censure or legal repercussions
- Fox hunters could combine sex and violence in their favourite sport
- Hedgehogs are gagging for it; you know they are
- It would liven up *One Man and His Dog*
- Two hundred years ago, they said that manned flight was 'unnatural . . .'
- People could cruise Battersea Dogs' Home looking for 'a bit of ruff'

THE BIBLE — why no publisher would touch it today

- It's by an unknown author
- There are far too many characters — and nowhere near enough sex

- It's the same old storyline of good versus evil
- The plot doesn't make sense
- And nobody would believe it
- The author keeps employing *deus ex machina*
- There are no plans for a follow-up
- The author won't plug it on *Wogan* or do any signings
- Religious books don't sell
- They'd worry the Philistines would sue for defamation of character (if any of them knew how to read)

THE BIRCH — why we should bring it back

- Lots of white, middle-class crimes would be solved when ex-public schoolboys flocked to police stations to confess
- Birchings could be videotaped and sold abroad as hardcore S & M movies, helping the British film industry to revive itself
- It would attract lots of new recruits into the police force
- They could broadcast the best birchings on *Crimewatch*
- It's kinder than four policemen repeatedly kidney-punching a suspect in a cell
- Birching is so flexible; the level of birching you received could be in direct proportion to your crime. For petty thieving, you could have six strokes with a knotted bundle of birch twigs; for murder, you could have an entire birch tree dropped on your head . . .
- The blood drawn from the birching could be donated to our hard-pressed blood transfusion service

BIRTH CONTROL — names for condoms sanctioned by Pope John Paul

- Moses Mambas — for when you enter the Promised Land
- Thy Kingdom Come ribbed slimfits
- Featherlite Goliaths — for the bigger man
- Torquemada Huggers — for the next time you use your poker
- Temptations — for the next time Satan gets behind thee
- Father, Son & Holy Ghost gossamers — packet of three
- Cardinal Sin lubricated sheaths

BLOOD DONOR — why you should never consider being one

- In America you get paid good cash for your blood — in this cheapo, cheapo country, you're lucky if you end up with a cold cup of Typhoo and a Sainsbury's own-brand digestive
- You pay prescription charges, but the NHS thinks *you* should give *them* things free
- As Julian Clary might say, 'No one enjoys a little prick'
- Even if you're a really rare blood type you get treated the same
- It *starts* with blood but next thing you know they're forcing you to sign a consent form to donate your retinas or spleen
- While you're donating blood the nurses are rifling your jacket pockets for any loose change
- The enamel badge you get after donating 25 pints looks really cheap
- Your blood probably wouldn't even go to people in NHS hospitals. At the end of a busy day at the clinic, they probably cram a couple of suit-cases full of prime Rhesus Negative bags and

jump on the first plane to the States to sell it for a fortune

BLOOD SPORTS — some new ideas

- High altitude frog bombing
- Fish tank mass electrocution
- Stuffing a guinea pig in a mincer (not very sporting, but strangely satisfying)
- Hamster stamping
- Hedgehog flame-throwing (in season only)
- Surface-to-air mallard-seeking missiles

BLUE PETER — where the charity appeal money should have gone in the 1970s

- 1971: The search to find a Petra lookalike after the original ran in front of a BBC OB unit
- 1972: The cameraman's sex-change operation
- 1973: Furnishing the floor manager's love nest
- 1974: Bribing the auditors to forget about 1973
- 1975: The Director General's pay rise
- 1976: Compensation due to Goldie's tragic 'error of judgement'
- 1977: The Director General's pay rise
- 1978: One of the presenter's divorce settlements
- 1979: Buying the negatives of that incident involving Shep and 'a close friend' at the end-of-series party

BOOK-BURNING — why it's a good thing

- You have to buy 'em to burn 'em
- It prevents copies being sold through second-hand shops when no author's royalties are paid
- It would be a tragedy if, 100 years from now, a Jeffrey Archer novel still existed
- Any book that's publicly burned automatically sells millions out of curiosity value. (Anyone

want to set light to this one on prime time TV? Please?)

- You can toast marshmallows and hold a Christian service at the same time
- It helps the illiterate to feel involved in the world of the written word, if only in a peripheral way
- Without it, there would be no literary criticism shows on Chilean television
- You can express your sense of outrage without declaring a fatwah (usually)
- It's an alternative natural-based fuel source and therefore very ecologically sound

BOXING — why it shouldn't be banned

- It's not often that you get the chance to be punched in the face and get paid for it
- If it weren't for boxing, gum-shield manufacturers would have gone to the wall years ago
- The urge to severely hurt one another is buried deep within our DNA and any attempt to suppress it would be going against the laws of nature
- People who want to box are brain damaged already so a few clouts to the head won't make much difference
- Boxing promoters/managers would be forced to take up some other activity equally suited to their personalities — like hare coursing, dog fighting or pimping
- Brain-stem injuries are a very under-researched area of medical science and we need all the victims we can get
- Without boxing Mike Tyson wouldn't have an incentive to behave in prison and get parole
- Frank Bruno would be forced to appear in panto all the time

BRAIN-DRAIN — why anyone with any sense or brains is getting out of Britain

- The education system is crap
- The country is crap
- The pay is crap
- The tax rates are crap
- The quality of life is crap
- Government funding is crap
- Government is crap
- Rewards for success are crap
- Recognition of achievement is crap
- Life in old age is worse than crap

BRAWN — why it's better than brain

- You can't see brain rippling through a tight T-shirt (unless you're on drugs)
- Having a Masters degree in Geography won't be much help if you're set upon by a thug with a snooker cue
- Arnold Schwarzenegger earns more in one week than Albert Einstein did in his entire life
- No one with an IQ of over 70 has ever won the World Wrestling Federation Championship
- Who got the most girls: Captain Kirk or Mr Spock?
- If *Rocky* had been written about a chess player it would not have enjoyed the same success
- No one ever got bullied at school for being strong

BREAST IMPLANTS — why they should be compulsory

- They just should, OK?

BRITISH NATIONAL PARTY — why it's good to be one of their parliamentary candidates

- If you don't have a car to tour the constituency in, your party workers could steal one for you
- You could identify with the problems of adult illiteracy, illegitimacy and unemployment because you fall into all three categories yourself
- There's no chance of you getting out of your depth during political debates at the party HQ
- A criminal record is probably an asset, not a liability
- The only qualifications are probably tattoos, an ugly wife and an Alsatian — not a father in politics or a big inheritance
- Disputes within the party are likely to be settled with a broken bottle, not some complicated ballot system
- You don't need to understand the arguments for or against proportional representation
- If you lose your deposit someone in the party will possibly mug an old lady and get it back

BSE — how we should tackle this dreadful mental disease in cattle

- Keep very quiet and pretend it's all over and gone away
- Give the affected cattle ECT or electro-convulsive therapy, thus ingeniously curing them and cooking them at the same time
- Reveal to the world that it's all just an evil hoax perpetrated by *vegetarians*
- Make sure the Secretary of State for Agriculture is seen to bite into a hamburger — just so long as he has an opportunity to spit it out again in secret
- Demonstrate scientifically that it cannot be

passed on to humans — by altering the
scientific findings
- Don't mention milk

BULLFIGHTING — why it must continue

- The bulls enjoy the sense of occasion
- How else will picadors earn a living?
- It enables the matadors to prove just how macho
  they are
- Without bullfighting we'd be robbed of the
  spectacle of watching a man in a purple satin
  costume and funny hat sticking swords in a
  bull's shoulders
- Hemingway knew a good thing when he saw it
- The bulls are going to die anyway and they
  might as well go out in a blaze of glory than
  squealing in some dirty old abattoir
- The bulls have a sporting chance; it's not as if
  they're sitting targets
- It brings in revenue to Spain; money that can be
  used to build bigger and better bull rings
- The bulls deserve to die; they're a menace
  running through those narrow streets in
  Pamplona
- It's not as if it's illegal

BUMPER STICKERS — some offensive and inciteful slogans

- Nuke the whale
- I stop for horses (then mutilate them)
- Unwanted baby on board
- Incontinent people do it in their sleep
- Honk if you're joyriding too
- If you can read this — you're not a policeman
- I ♥ Iraq
- The unemployed are workshy
- Euthanasia now!

- Santa doesn't exist
- Save fuel — burn pets
- Friends of Sellafield
- Give blood — let me run you over
- Vote Conservative

BURGLARS — how to take effective action against the scourge of the 1990s

- Write to your local MP and demand that school holidays be abolished
- Phone up your local zoo and offer your house as a holiday home for their entire collection of venomous snakes and boa constrictors
- Leave a bottle of finest blended malt whisky somewhere the burglar can't fail to notice it, having first blended it with plenty of sulphuric acid
- Run an electrical charge through your carpet so the instant the burglar pisses on it (which he invariably will), his genitals will resemble crispy bacon
- Tell everyone you're going on holiday — then spend two weeks secretly crouched behind the sofa with an AK47 and night vision goggles
- Take all of your decent CDs out of their cases and replace them with copies of Rolf Harris albums (guaranteed to get the burglar duffed up while selling them in the pub)
- Paint a huge red cross on your door and write 'Bubonic plague; may the Lord have mercy on all our souls' underneath it
- Beat up anyone selling electrical goods at car boot sales the moment you spot them
- Before going on holiday, sell all your electrical goods at a car boot sale, then go home, tip out all your drawers, crap on your bed, rip up all the photographs you have of your dead parents and piss up the walls of your living room — thus

26

leaving genuine burglars at a loose end when they do break in . . .

BUS SEATS — why you shouldn't give up yours to an old lady

- You paid; she's got a free bus pass
- She expects you to — and life should still be full of surprises, even at 70
- You got there first
- She wouldn't give up her seat for you
- You're exhausted from a hard day's work, while she's just probably wombled around the shops a bit
- When the bus turns a corner, she'll go flying and it'll be a good laugh
- She can balance perfectly well standing up with her zimmer frame
- She's had her life; now it's your turn to enjoy yourself

CAPITALISM — big business opportunities in Russia today

- Open up a franchise called 'Turnips U Like'
- Or 'Kentucky Fried Cat'
- Or the dead-rat-on-a-stick concession in Moscow Central Station
- Charge people twenty roubles apiece just to handle some fruit
- Buy the entire country for about $700 and sell its people into slavery (it's not as if they're not used to it)
- Gain the sole rights to promote Alcoholics Anonymous there
- Open up an all-night cabbage-burger joint
- Get respected heroes of the Great Patriotic War to endorse your bath scourer
- Sell the contents of your dustbin to mile-long queues in Red Square market
- Bring over your scratched and unloved Herman's Hermits and Dave Clark Five albums, which are the ultimate status symbols for the with-it Muscovite

28

CAPITALISM — bad business ventures in Russia today

- Trying to sell anything that costs more than 5p
- Offering limited edition prints of Lenin
- Or Boris Yeltsin
- Having the sole rights to alcohol-free lagers
- Bikinis
- Beauty salons — as a race, they're beyond all hope

CARS — good politically incorrect things to shout from them

- 'You got a couple of spacehoppers in there, luv?'
- 'Get your lips round my Lewis Collins, darlin'!'
- 'Show us your white bits!'
- 'Wannnnkkkkerrrrrrrr!'
- 'Are you a virgin?'
- 'Do you like chicken, love? Well, suck this — it's foul!'
- 'Hey darlin', you look just like Sonia!'
- 'Like my bum?'
- 'I like your tits!'
- 'Climb in and climb on!'

CATALYTIC CONVERTORS — what a waste of time

- You have to take the car dealer's word that one's been fitted
- It doesn't make the car go any faster
- Or even sound any faster
- In fact, it'll knacker its performance
- It's not as flashy as a spoiler
- What's the point of paying extra for something on a car that you can't even see?
- If someone asks you what it does exactly, you won't know
- If you don't have any kids why bother about lead pollution in the atmosphere?

- It doesn't stop carbon monoxide, so you're still pumping out lots of shit every day
- Why would you ever want to convert a 'catalytic'?

CAVEMEN — why they make excellent role models for today's politically incorrect masses

- They didn't care that the sabre-tooth tiger or woolly mammoth was an endangered species; they just went out and killed it
- Courtship rituals were short, brutal and to the point, a tradition still continued on many council estates to this day
- They too spoke in a series of guttural, meaningless grunts
- The strongest, most ruthless caveman was king. Now that's how to elect a government. In prehistoric times, John Major would be at the back of the cave, scavenging for leftovers with the old women
- They worshipped rocks and rock stratum. Now we worship diamonds and rock bands
- If you were a vegetarian back then, you'd have starved
- If you fell ill, you were left on a hillside to die. Much cheaper than the modern NHS — and about as effective
- If you had any liberal ideas whatsoever, your tribe would sacrifice you to the local volcano god
- They used to paint on walls as well

CENSORSHIP — why it's a good thing

- It lets ▬▬ ▬▬ ▬▬ dead
- The ▬▬▬ ▬▬ been ▬▬▬ ▬▬ police
- Some of ▬▬ ▬▬ ▬▬ cut
- No one's ▬▬▬ ▬▬ ▬▬ any ▬▬ literature

- Prince ▬▬ won't ▬▬ ▬▬ ▬ Di's ▬ hole

THE CHATTERING CLASSES — why don't they shut up?

- Because, like, it's like rilly, rilly important to talk things through, yah?
- They have nothing better to do with their lives
- They think they can solve the world's problems with a series of dinner parties for close friends
- Like, today's *Guardian* rilly raised some valid points, yah?
- If they did, they'd become part of the silent majority and that would be just too, too vulgar, yah?
- The opinions formed by the Chattering Classes today are vital in fucking up our country tomorrow, OK?
- If they stopped chattering for just a second, people would realise what crap they were spouting
- They're already idle; at least their mouths are doing something
- Radio 4 would be bloody quiet and the *Late Show* wouldn't exist

CHESTY BABES — why they're valuable members of society

- They keep the R & D departments of bra manufacturers on their toes
- When they wear low cut dresses they keep everyone else on their toes
- They make it easy when you're interviewing loads of candidates for a job
- They're good for the economy (thousands of people are employed in the pin-up calendar, porn video and girlie-magazine industries)
- The fact that they make flat-chested women

31

insecure keeps plastic surgeons busy and provides a welcome boost for the silicon industry
- They provoke scientific discussion (like questioning whether Newton was 100 per cent right about gravity)
- Without them, the *Benny Hill Show* would have been about seven minutes long (including the commercials)
- They give the *Sun* something to print
- *Baywatch* could not be made without them

CHILD LABOUR — why industry should welcome its return

- If they fall into heavy machinery there's less of them to scrape out
- It doesn't matter if they work a 15-hour shift because there's no school the next day
- They won't understand the concepts of trade unions, minimum wages or the Health and Safety Executive
- You'll never have to pay maternity leave (except in a few cases . . .)
- You can increase productivity by threatening them with the bogie man who lives in the stationery cupboard
- Or by giving them loads of blue Smarties
- Disciplinary action can take the form of detention rather than some industrial tribunal

CHILDREN — why boys and girls *should* be brought up differently

- A boy with an interest in cookery will not survive his first term at school
- A boy dressed in pink will not survive his first day at school

32

- Boys should never be allowed to use lipstick — unless as Red Indian warpaint
- A girl given a junior ironing board is learning a positive social skill which will stand her in good stead when finding a husband
- Boys who have an interest in dolls and junior vacuum cleaners may well turn out to be New Men in later life
- Boys look silly in frilly ribbons and bows
- Boys should be brought up to fight and cuss like real men; girls brought up the same way are likely to find themselves in psychiatric care
- A girl who shows early promise with a football might well end up playing in a woman's football team — and you don't want her mixing with *that sort*
- A girl who likes playing with toy soldiers might end up in the Women's Army — and you certainly don't want her mixing with *that sort*
- Boys who are treated the same as their sisters might grow up with all kinds of odd notions about equality

CHILDREN — how to answer your child's difficult questions

- 'Shut up'
- 'Cos it is'
- 'Cos I say so'
- 'Ask your mother'
- 'Oy, don't get lippy'
- 'Go and watch the telly'
- 'Don't ask stupid questions'
- 'Don't know, don't care'
- 'You want the back of my hand?'
- 'Oy, I'm watchin' telly, all right?'
- 'Shove off!'
- 'Bugger off!'
- 'Sod off!'

- 'Piss off!'
- 'Fuck off!'

CHILE — things it buys from the West that make it a valuable trading ally

- Devices that deliver an electrical charge to the genitals
- Devices that deliver an electrical charge to every other part of the body
- Phone-tapping equipment
- Sodium pentathol
- Pliers
- Chloroform
- Things you wouldn't want anywhere near your rectum
- 200-watt bulbs for desk lamps
- Tape recorders
- Silence

CHURCH — things it has real trouble explaining

- Terminal illnesses
- Air crashes
- Widespread famine and poverty
- Why we should believe in an afterlife when there's absolutely no evidence for it
- Wars
- Pain and suffering
- People cut down in the prime of life
- Flying saucers
- Mick Hucknall's face
- God

THE CIA — 10 ways they could raise money to fight the covert war in South America, rather than smuggling drugs

- CIA charity shops in the high street
- Selling raffle tickets (first prize, the assassination of the person of your choice)
- Baking cookies and selling them door to door
- Sponsored coups
- Bob-A-Dirty-Job week
- Shaking a collection box on the street corner ('Please give generously: fourteen fascist dictators and a dozen death squads to support')
- Hold a CIA rag week in which a dozen secret agents dressed as naughty nurses push a giant coffin through the streets, spray everyone with crazy string and publish a magazine full of racist jokes about Libyans
- Use their big black limos for car boot sales
- Sell all their secrets to Cuba

CIGARETTES — some perfectly good reasons to smoke

- Every packet you buy provides tax for the government to pay for new hospitals
- Smoking keeps people who make lighters and matches in work
- It also keeps people who make cigarettes in work
- You *know* that you can beat the odds
- You've always fancied playing Russian roulette — and you don't own a gun
- Dot Cotton smokes and she's your role model
- You've got white wallpaper at home — and you'd rather it was marigold (ish)
- It's good for your nerves (until you see one of those Health Education films, or it's 11.30 on a Sunday night and you've run out)

- If you didn't smoke, bums wouldn't be able to pick up dog ends from the gutter
- Smoking keeps the Benson & Hedges Snooker Championship going — and without that BBC2 would have nothing to show 300 days of the year
- You can impress all your mates at school
- When life assurance questionnaires ask if you smoke, you'll be able to write 'YES' and proudly cough up more
- You'll never need to waste money on Nicorette patches or hypnotherapy
- They can do wonders with chemotherapy nowadays

CIRCUS ANIMALS — the classic acts of yesteryear they should bring back

- Edwina, the marmoset cannonball
- Lennie, the sub-aqua badger
- Binkie and Pinkie, the fire-walking squirrels
- Bruin, motorcycle stunt bear extraordinaire
- George and Georgina, the knife-throwing chimpanzees
- Hector, the flying llama
- Blackie, the bungee-jumping Alsatian
- Dobbin, pony in a centrifuge

CLONING — why cloning is a good idea

- We can all have our own personal Kim Basinger
- Or Arnold Schwarzenegger
- Or even Jonathan Ross, if that's your bag
- We can all have our own personal clones — and use them when we need a donor organ, with no fear of rejection problems
- Bruce Springsteen could tour in every major city in the world — simultaneously
- You could commit terrible crimes before

hundreds of witnesses — and simply blame
your clone
- You could have sex with yourself — and *really*
find out how good you are in bed

COAL MINES — why they should be shut down

- Miners get all kinds of terrible lung diseases
- They're dangerous places to work
- Miners come off shift looking like vicious racial
stereotypes
- Many mines are in Wales, so that's reason
enough in itself
- There'll be no more bloody boring colliery brass
bands or massed voice choirs
- Whole communities will be put on the dole,
making DSS administration very simple and
cost-effective
- To give our European partners a chance to sell
to our market
- To make way for the undisputed dominance of
nuclear power

'COMIC RELIEF' — 5 reasons not to give

- The last red plastic thing you stuck on your car
scratched the paint
- Famine relief is the last thing on your mind
when you see French and Saunders
- You've seen funnier sketches on a war artist's
pad
- You've heard a rumour that all the money they
raise will go towards making a new series of
The Comic Strip (which is the last thing that
anybody wants)
- The BBC puts it on instead of your favourite
programme

COMMON PEOPLE — the wit and wisdom of the working class as revealed in a typical conversation

- A: I was down the pub the other night, right?
- B: Right
- A: An' this geezer, right, one of Gazza's mates, right, he goes, 'right', he goes . . .
- B: Yeah?
- A: So I goes, 'right', right? I goes, I goes, I go, 'right', I go, yeah?
- B: Yeah
- A: So I goes, right, I fucking goes 'right', right? An' he goes, he goes some old bollocks, right, he goes?
- B: Yeah
- A: I goes 'right', right? And I'm goin' like and he comes back and he goes and gives it some of that and I goes, 'Don't you give it some of that with me', right?
- B: Right. All mouth he is.
- A: So I goes, I go, right, I go, all right then, I goes. 'Go on then' and he goes, he goes, 'right?' He goes . . . 'Yeah?', right, so I goes . . .

(*I think the readers get the point — ed.*)

COMMUNITY POLICE OFFICERS — some politically incorrect things to say to them

- 'I earn more in an hour than you take home a week, mate!'
- 'That's a funny helmet you got there!'
- 'Th-th-that's all, folks!'
- 'Oy, copper! Didn't I see you on *Mastermind* last night?'
- 'Look, it's Reg Hollis!'
- 'That reminds me, lads, I'm dying for a packet of pork scratchings'
- 'The modern judicial system! The modern

judicial system!' (They hate this — it makes them feel completely impotent)
- 'Ha! I'm innocent. You can't touch me'. (This confuses them)

CONCESSIONARY RAIL FARES — why we should discontinue them

- Who wants to listen to the noise of screaming kids or clacking knitting needles anyway?
- Less old people on the train means a better chance of finding a toilet that's vacant and clean
- Trains will be much safer without young mothers blocking the aisles with pushchairs
- It saves us from having Gary Glitter staring down at us from posters
- It'll teach old people to live nearer their grandchildren so they can babysit
- It teaches people not to take things for granted

CONSCIENTIOUS OBJECTORS — why they're big sissies

- They're scared about being shot by the enemy
- Or being captured and tortured — then shot
- Or being caught in friendly fire incidents two minutes after the battle starts
- Or accidentally treading on a landmine
- Or catching red-hot shrapnel in the bollocks
- Or watching their best friend get hit full in the face by a fragmentation grenade
- Or having to machine-gun innocent civilians
- Or being forgotten by a fickle public when stuck in a wheelchair and begging
- Or suffering from Post Traumatic Stress Disorder eight months after a battle
- Or having unnatural things done to their bottoms during Army initiation ceremonies

COUNCIL ESTATES — why your local estate should be nuked

- School league tables in the area would improve drastically
- You'd be able to come out of your house in the morning and find your car aerial still attached to your car
- It would be a pretty fair bet that you could enjoy an evening without two morons fighting, pissing or puking in your garden after closing time
- Your children would have to travel much further afield to buy their crack
- Dole queues would be slashed at a stroke
- All the local kebab shops would close down, thus stopping the trail of discarded greasy paper, half-masticated lumps of pitta bread and green slivers of lettuce leading all the way up your road to the estate
- The nuclear family would once more be the norm
- There are too many plasterers and electricians in the world as it is
- The police wouldn't have to worry about Operation Bumblebee any more
- You'd never see a pit bull terrier again

COUNTRY BUMPKINS — things they say

- 'Arr'
- 'Arr, I be roight bored, I be'
- 'Arr, I think oi'll go off an' live in the big city'
- 'Arr, but then who'd mind the sheep?'
- 'Arr, bugger the sheep'
- 'Arr, but oi'd miss that, I would . . .'
- 'Arr, I think I'll be staying here a mite longer'
- 'Arr, come here, Fluffy, me love'
- 'Arr, Arr! Arr! Arr! ARR!'

- 'Arr, wuz it good for 'ee too?'

CONVICTED CRIMINALS — how to ensure they never want to see the inside of a prison again

- Make it compulsory to touch their toes in the showers at least twice a day
- Paint a big target on their bottoms
- Run a harmless but painful electric charge through their slopping out bucket, so that every time they relieve themselves it's agony
- Make them wear frilly French maid's outfits
- Have the TV in the leisure room permanently tuned to BBC2
- Offer the same menu, morning, noon and night, 365 days a year
- Tie their testicles securely to the landing rail and then tip them over on to the safety nets below — at least five times a day
- Invite The Chippendales to put on a regular show there
- Make them wear balls and chains around their ankles — the balls being still attached to one of their cellmates
- Have piped Muzak in all the cells

CYCLISTS — 10 reasons why cyclists should be banned from the road

- They wobble precariously every time you sweep past them at 80 mph
- They look stupid
- Many of them are 'vegetarians' as well
- They tinkle irritating little bells at you
- Half the time, you never see them until they're sprawled across your bonnet
- They weave in and out when you're stuck, fuming in a traffic jam, with inane 'vegetarian' grins all over their faces

- They don't pay road tax
- They think that having a couple of gears on their bikes makes them major athletes
- They pull alongside you at the traffic lights and scratch your paintwork with their handlebars
- Those bright purple day-glo cycling shorts make them look like members of Erasure (and reveal far more than you want to see)

DEAF PEOPLE — what to say to offend them

- Anything you like

DEMOCRACY — why we should abandon it

- It keeps returning the Conservatives to power
- Stupid people are allowed to vote along with the intelligent (see above)
- One person, one vote is bound to favour the lowest common denominator
- To win popularity in a democracy, politicians must promise policies which will appeal to the mob, no matter how much they might damage the nation
- America's a democracy — and do we really want to end up like that?
- Politicans who want to rule the country should be made to battle it out in an 'arena of death' to see who's the strongest. (Mind you, this would probably see the return of Margaret Thatcher)
- The European Community is run by unelected bureaucrats — and that's bloody good, so our leaders keep telling us

- Things couldn't be any worse under any other system
- Fascism makes for much more dynamic government
- 1,008,200,000 Chinese can't all be wrong

DEVIL WORSHIP — why it's good

- You get to dance naked with members of the opposite sex without having to put an ad in *Forum* magazine
- You never need to go to church on Sunday mornings
- You can sacrifice the neighbour's cat that's always pissing on your prize rhododendrons
- You don't need to obey, let alone remember, the Ten Commandments
- You can earn extra money by selling your soul
- It gives you the chance to practise your O-level geometry every time you draw a pentangle
- You're not racked with guilt every time you do something nasty
- You understand why there's so much suffering and tragedy in the world

DISABILITY BENEFIT — things claimants should have to do in order to prove their entitlement

- Walk barefoot across burning coals
- Wrestle with a brown bear — and win
- Bungee jump
- Enter an internationally recognised kick-boxing championship and reach at least the quarter finals
- Do a Cossack dance
- Complete a half-marathon on a pogo stick
- Copy all Michael Jackson's footwork in the 'Thriller' video

- Tread water for 25 minutes in the local swimming baths
- Juggle five blazing torches while riding a unicycle
- Play football for England alongside the ten other players claiming disability benefit

DISASTERS — why it's good to have a huge chemical disaster in a Third World country

- At worst, you'll have to pay a fiver in compensation to each of the families of those killed
- At best, you can slip the local governor a tenner and he'll prevent criminal charges being brought against your company
- If you kill a thousand people in the Third World, you'll only get a ten-second slot, maximum, on *News at Ten*, minimising the bad publicity
- It's easy to replace the dead workers with people desperate for their jobs — at even lower wages
- Chances are, you won't kill anyone from a family with enough money to sue you properly (or even to buy a postage stamp to write to complain)
- If the wind takes the toxic fumes, it'll just spill into another Third World country, instead of somewhere important
- You won't have anyone important from your company on-site in a shithole like that

DIRTY JOKES — punchlines to some of the best

- 'Nobody eats parsley!'
- 'Kermit's finger!'
- 'But if I rub it, it turns into a briefcase!'
- 'You can only fit three fingers in a bowling ball!'
- 'So you can floss after you eat!'
- 'A liquor licence'

45

- 'He could read lips!'
- 'Roll her in flour and go for the wet spot!'
- 'So that when you're drunk you can carry them home like a six-pack'
- 'And he uses it to brush the au pair's teeth'

DIVORCE — 10 good reasons to chuck the missus

- Impulse
- Boredom
- You're fed up with her living in the battered women's refuge
- Meeting a 17-year-old nymphet who actually likes sexually inadequate paunchy menopausal men
- To make sure your children don't have it too easy growing up
- Your mates are all doing it
- She's put on at least 5 lb since you married her
- Your horoscope says it's time for a big change in your domestic situation
- Why keep your old car if you can get a newer model?
- You fancy living in a bedsitter and paying 80 per cent of your wages in alimony for the rest of your life

DIVORCE — why it's good for children

- They get two sets of presents each birthday and Christmas
- Both parents try to out-do each other when it comes to outings at the weekends
- They get the chance to vet any potential step-parent
- They learn all about manipulation when they play one parent off against the other
- They can sympathise with the Royal grandchildren

- Teachers will make allowances for them doing appallingly in their GCSEs
- They get a day off school when they have to go to court in the custody battle
- It gives them an excuse for screwing their own life up when they're older

DOG FIGHTING — why it should be legalised

- Every dog killed is one less dangerous dog in the country
- It's not as if *people* are getting ripped to shreds
- It's not as if the dogs don't want to fight
- It's a dog-eat-dog world out there
- The purchase of dog-fighting licences will generate extra income for local councils
- Fox hunting is legal

DOGS OF WAR — why it's more exciting to be an international mercenary than a Kelly Girl temp

- You get sent on assignments to exciting places like Bosnia and Somalia rather than the Elephant and Castle or 'just off Staples Corner'
- You get to use anti-tank bazookas instead of IBM compatibles
- No one tells you to make tea for them — and if they do, you just shoot them in the head
- You don't have to dress smartly but casually — just ensure you have a necklace of severed ears around your neck
- When temping you may be called upon to deal with difficult members of the public; mercenaries have a wider choice of responses at their disposal
- Kelly Girl require good references; to be accepted as a mercenary, all you have to say is 'I was with Mad Mitch in the Congo' or 'I've just finished a ten stretch' and you're in

- No one in your unit cares about your P45, whereas at Kelly Girl you immediately go on to emergency tax for a thousand weeks until someone can be bothered to sort it out
- You never have to worry about being out of work — even when there's a recession on, there's still a war happening somewhere in the world

THE DOLE — why it should be scrapped

- If it was scrapped, no one would be able to fiddle it
- The unemployed could then be forced to work in sweatshops for a pittance, making us highly competitive against Third World imports for a change
- We don't get paid enough to subsidise the sick, the lazy and the unskilled
- If people knew there was no unemployment benefit it might encourage them to work harder and avoid getting fired
- Instead of signing on, people could use that time to look for work
- It would prevent DSS clerks being assaulted by irate claimants
- Because people today don't know how cushy life is
- The figures for those claiming benefit would be slashed by three million at a stroke — making the Government look brilliant and caring
- Most of the people on the dole are already making a living begging in the streets anyway
- Scousers are scum

DOLPHINS — reasons why they're stupid

- They keep swimming into bloody big tuna nets which you can see a mile off

- They call their kids things like 'Flipper'
- They insist on living off the coast of Japan — which is a big mistake for *any* form of marine life
- They demonstrate their alleged intelligence by jumping through hoops and balancing balls on their noses (and athletes are not renowned for their intellectual prowess)
- Not one dolphin has ever got their GCSE woodwork, let alone qualified for MENSA
- They have holes in the top of their heads
- They're willing to perform at dolphinariums for a bucket of fish, rather than a percentage of the gross
- Their language consists entirely of squeaks and whistles
- They trust people
- They smile a lot

DONOR ORGANS — why we should get them from Third World citizens

- Market forces — only the rich can afford them; only the poorest want to sell them
- Who needs *two* kidneys anyway?
- They're cheap and plentiful
- It beats having to wait for a car crash
- Where else can we get such a plentiful supply?

DOCTOR WHO — politically unsound things he could say

- 'Look at the tits on that Ogron!'
- 'I reckon we should send all the Cybermen back to where they came from'
- 'Daleks have those big families and then expect the State to look after them'
- 'What do you call a Kroton in a suit? — The accused!'

- 'There was this Zarbi, this Dominator and this Sea Devil in a bar, right?'
- 'How many Silurians does it take to change a light bulb?'
- 'Don't get many of those to the pound, Leela!'
- 'Hey Ace! Let's go Ice Warrior bashing!'
- 'Yeti scum! They come over here, take our jobs, marry our women . . .'
- 'You Sontaran benders make me sick!'
- 'What do you say to a Zygon with a job, Jo? — Big Mac and large fries please'

DRUGS — why they should be legalised

- Because then the cartels would have to deal with VAT and corporation tax and National Insurance and banks ripping them off and they'd go under in months, like most legitimate businesses are doing

DYSLEXIC — what the term *really* means

- Thick
- Stupid
- Idiotic
- Brainless
- Dense
- Dim
- Veggie
- Moronic
- Retarded
- Half-witted

EARTH — proof that it isn't a living entity as some politically correct thinkers claim

- It doesn't go 'Ouch!' when you stand on it or sink a gardening fork into it
- All living things excrete — but no one has ever detected 'planetary poohs' in our orbit
- The Earth revolves at an amazing speed; if it were alive, it would get dizzy and fall off its axis
- If it were alive, surely it would have the urge to reproduce and set off to shag Venus
- You'd hear it snoring at night
- People have claimed that the Earth or 'Gaia' is female and that the Himalayas are its breasts and the Grand Canyon its vagina — but they're safely locked up now, so you can sleep soundly tonight
- Space has no air in it, so how could a living planet breathe?
- It doesn't get taxed

EDUCATION — what a more liberal education policy will undoubtedly lead to

- 100 per cent absenteeism
- A 100 per cent rise in the amount of thieving from local shopkeepers
- A generation of total functional illiterates who are all committed socialists and understand what Diwali represents, but not what two plus two equals
- Double Sega on Tuesday afternoons
- Double-beating the shit out of first years every day of the week
- Double smoking every day of the week
- Double shagging in the stationery cupboard
- Double teacher-bashing — a healthy form of self-expression
- A generation of savage little sociopaths with the moral grasp of Adolf Hitler and the sense of social empathy of Peter Sutcliffe
- An eventual return to the Stone Age

THE ELDERLY — politically incorrect things to do to a sweet old lady

- Shoot her point blank with a high velocity hunting rifle
- Dress up as the Grim Reaper and make a surprise entrance at 4 a.m.
- Buy her a nice retirement flat — in Bosnia
- Trick her into taking up advanced aerobics
- Make dead of night telephone calls claiming to be the restless spirit of her beloved son George, who disappeared over the polders in his Wellington in 1941
- Attach castors to her zimmer frame
- Creep up behind her and yell as loudly as you can, 'Take cover! It's a doodlebug!'
- Offer to escort her across the road — and then

leave her to fend for herself halfway across a frantically busy dual carriageway pulsating with Eurojuggernauts

YOUR ELDERS — why you shouldn't respect them

- They're rude and grumpy and push in front of you in the bus queue
- They think Victor Sylvester and Syd Lawrence are scorching hot
- You can duff them up, easy
- So they fought in the war? Big deal
- They're full of crap advice, which might have had some use before the advent of powered flight, but . . .
- They've had their lives — and fucked them up, judging by their state of poverty and near destitution now
- They like the Royal Family
- Times change — unlike their underwear
- How can you take someone wearing incontinence knickers seriously?

ELECTIONS — reasons for banning them

- It saves having to close the schools on polling day and disrupting children's valuable education
- Candidates won't have to waste their time campaigning and kissing smelly babies
- The streets will be a much quieter place without cars with loudspeakers on their roofs
- No one can be accused of rigging the results
- You won't be pestered by opinion polls asking who you support
- It prevents our normal TV programmes being interrupted by 'Election Specials'
- No one will catch a cold standing outside their

town hall at 3 a.m. waiting for the results to be announced
- It prevents people suffering from claustrophobia worrying about standing in a polling booth
- There's no point because the same party always wins

ELECTRIC CARS — reasons why they're crap

- If you drive them in the rain you might get a shock
- Even bicycles can burn you up
- By not using any petrol you won't be able to save up vouchers for glass tumblers and other worthwhile gifts
- Imagine having to check the levels of 124 batteries
- You couldn't go for a drive with a hot date and pretend you've run out of petrol
- If you desperately wanted something with a top speed of 25 mph and a range of 30 miles you'd buy a Skoda
- Does the term 'C5' ring a bell?

ELECTRIC CHAIR — why it's a good idea

- It can curl your hair if it's straight
- It can straighten your hair if it's curly
- It's also good for removing unwanted hair
- It dims the lights all over Death Row, making it perfect for the inmates to get all smoochy and in the mood with each other
- It's a boost for the electricity company shareholders
- It's more effective than a clockwork chair
- And more humane than a chair-with-a-six-inch-skewer-pointing-upwards-from-the-seat into which the condemned man is slowly lowered

- It can start your heart again if you're clinically dead (but not for long)
- You can connect a set of jumps leads to it and help start your car
- It slashes recidivism rates drastically

ELEPHANTS — why you should shoot them

- You can't miss
- There'll be one less big-nosed grey bastard in the world
- They eat more than their fair share of sticky buns
- They have huge flapping ears and a scattering of hairs on their head — so you could practise on them first for your assassination attempt on Prince Charles
- Because they're there . . . at least now; wait another ten years and you might never get the chance to 'bag' one
- You'd feel stupid shooting an ant
- An elephant's head looks more impressive on the wall of your trophy room than a hamster's head
- Elephants are so thick that, when you shoot one, its mate stays around for hours crying instead of pissing off sharpish like any sensible mammal — making it easy pickings to 'bag' a pair
- You could go down in history as the person who finally made the elephant extinct

ENDANGERED SPECIES OF THE TWENTIETH CENTURY

- The honest politician
- The honest anybody
- The intellectual

- The person who can write his own name in the ground with a stick
- Innocent old people enduring a living hell on council estates
- The driving instructor who doesn't try to touch up all his 17-year-old female pupils
- GPs who give a shit
- Someone possessed of a moral code
- Someone who knows what a moral code is
- The monarchy

ENERGY — some radical ways to save it

- Cut off the supply of anyone who can't afford to pay for it
- Refuse to sell petrol to anyone in a crap car
- Stop pensioners' free bus passes, so we'll need less buses on the road
- Ban the use of electric heaters in winter
- Put two council families into one council house so they can share the energy bill
- Make relatives pay for energy-consuming devices in hospitals — like life support machines. (Then we'll really see how much they care . . .)
- Put VAT on it (Oh, someone's already thought of that . . .)
- Privatise the energy companies so that bills skyrocket (Oh, someone's already thought of that too . . .)

EQUAL OPPORTUNITIES — jobs women will never do as well as men

- Male stripper
- Baritone singer
- Sperm donor
- Urinal tester
- Pacesetter in the men's 5,000 metres
- Elvis impersonator
- Rent boy
- King

EQUAL OPPORTUNITIES — jobs that women do much better than men

- Tea lady
- Blue movie actress
- Page 3 pin-up
- Waitress
- Housewife
- Tampon tester
- Wetnurse
- Lollipop lady
- French maid

EQUAL OPPORTUNITIES — professions which employ more than the usual quota of the challenged members of society

- Estate agents — compulsive liars
- Heathrow baggage handlers — kleptomaniacs
- Lawyers — wankers
- Accountancy — bores
- Garages — cretins
- Social services — social inadequates
- Art critics — the visually impaired
- Hospitals — loonies who pretend they're medically qualified
- Taxicab firms — sociopaths
- The higher judiciary — doddery old gits

EQUAL PAY — why it's a misguided concept

- Men are stronger than women and therefore better value for money
- Women do all the easy jobs
- Women spend more of the working day gossiping and going to the toilet than their male counterparts
- Men need to earn more than women, because a night on the piss doesn't come cheap
- If women were grossly underpaid, there'd be less of them in the workforce, allowing full male employment for the first time in decades

ESKIMOS — why they're stupid

- They look like Red Indians gone wrong
- They think that you kiss by rubbing noses (have they never heard of snot?)
- Their houses are made of blocks of ice
- They all wear parkas, making them look like a race of train spotters
- Rather than going to the local Kwik Save for their dinner they prefer to spend four days squatting around a hole in the ice
- They have 72 different words for snow when the rest of the world manages quite nicely with just one
- Their favourite food is polar bear
- Unfortunately, a polar bear's favourite food is Eskimo
- They rub seal blubber all over their skin to keep them warm (pooh!)
- They choose to live in the coldest, shittiest place in the whole world
- They prefer scrimshaw to watching videos
- They call themselves Inuits

ETHICAL INVESTMENTS — why they're a waste of money

- It must be said that soya and muesli are not amongst the world's most traded commodities
- When did you last see a company that makes organically farmed carrots in the FT Top 100 index?
- Most multinational corporations didn't get where they are today by not exploiting people, animals or natural resources
- Even a company manufacturing wheelchairs probably makes bits for Trident submarines
- Putting your life savings into Quorn is probably not a good idea

- Treating nuclear waste is far more profitable than treating patients

ETHIOPIA — why its government should spend money on weapons, not food

- Parading SS20 missiles through the streets of Addis Ababa is more impressive than parading two loaves of bread and a past-its-sell-by-date Mars bar
- It enables them to fight neighbouring countries for *their* food
- They can protect convoys of foreign aid as it arrives in the country
- If there is a border skirmish with Somalia, a soldier armed only with an apple is no match for a Kalashnikov
- If they change their minds about the weapons they can always beat them into ploughshares
- Guns last longer than food
- If they received food, they'd only trade it for guns anyway
- So they can keep their starving population under control
- And away from the secret government stash of caviar, smoked salmon and vintage champagne

EUROPE — a politically incorrect guide to the community

Brussels Headquarters of the EC. Also capital of Sproutland
Sir Leon Brittan 'Fatty Leon', a spotty, ugly, pompous British politician who is now a spotty, ugly, pompous European politician
Butter Mountain (See 'Sir Leon Brittan')
Jacques Delors Rhyming slang (Jacques Delors = Up Yours)

Democracy   I don't remember voting for Delors, do you?

ECU   Proposed single unit of currency for Europe. Unhappily, also Portuguese for 'bum'. You just know that changing over to ECUs is going to do to prices in the shops what decimalisation did — and that the Germans will still take home twice as many in their wage packets as you will

Euro MP   Appointed in the elections which nobody ever bothers to turn out for

European Industries   Why do all European companies have names like VAG and TAT and Siemens, and call their products Pschitt! and Sic! and 'Bum' crisps. Is this because of European laws on truth in advertising, or are they just different to us?

Federalism   Being told what to do by foreigners

Federal Subsidy   Giving your tax money to Frog farmers

Free Trade   Roast beef and Yorkshire pud will be banned and we'll all be eating yum-yum horse meat frankfurters and petit filous (whatever that is) and that Mullerrice stuff which they advertise on GMTV and which makes you want to puke when you see it

Maastricht Agreement   Unconditional surrender

Jacques Poos   Further proof that they're not like us

Referendum   Something they permit and then frantically try to ignore if it doesn't suit them. Further proof of Euro-Democracy in action

Single Market   Cheap fags and booze

Soixante-neuf   The only French phrase worth knowing

Margaret Thatcher   She knows what's what, mate

United Europe   Hitler's dream in 1939

EUROPEAN CULTURE — some reasons why it's the best in the world

- Topo Gigio
- The Eurovision Song Contest
- *Jeux Sans Frontières*
- Bavarian thigh-slapping dance extravaganzas
- That Italian quiz show where contestants have to take their clothes off
- The Smurfs
- Legoland
- Demis Roussos
- EuroDisney
- The German game show in which contestants win prizes according to the whim of a hamster called Willi
- Marcel Marceau
- Bullfighting

EUTHANASIA — why it should be made compulsory for anyone over 75

- It saves them worrying about dying from hypothermia during winter
- It saves their children worrying about the extortionate cost of keeping them in a rest home
- It's better than suggesting euthanasia for anyone *under* 75
- It saves them worrying about whether they're going to make it to their 76th birthday
- It will rid the world once and for all of toothless women with beards
- It's far more dignified than dying alone in a flat and the neighbours discovering the body because of its smell, 72 hours later
- You get the chance to organise a big knees-up farewell party with all your family

- You've got the chance to make sure that Tiddles is well provided for after your death
- Just one little injection can save the NHS and social services a fortune

EVIDENCE — why the police should falsify it

- Because they're not bright enough to find it
- It's like fiddling your expenses; everyone does it
- It saves them wading through loads of real evidence which might take ages to investigate (not to mention the paperwork it would entail)
- It enables the police to clear up more crimes, which is, after all, what they are there for
- It enables the accused to win huge amounts of damages when the truth eventually does come out — money they would never ordinarily see
- What's good enough for Middle Eastern dictators is good enough for us
- Barristers can get extra work by defending the police when they're convicted themselves
- The convicted can write best-selling books about their wrongful arrest and appear on TV chat shows
- There's no smoke without fire . . .

FASCIST DICTATORS — why it's good to be one

- You get to wear a snazzy military uniform
- Including loads and loads of medals
- And really good-looking skintight jodhpurs
- And shiny patent leather boots
- Girls will flock to you, irresistibly drawn to your power (or the skintight jodhpurs)
- You're your own boss
- No one dares complain if you oversleep, play your records loud or use bad language
- You can own loads of tanks and aircraft
- You can butcher thousands but still appear entertaining, lovable and fair
- You can go to a restaurant and order the death of fourteen dissident students then say, 'Silly me! I meant to order the steak tartare!'

FASHIONS — why women should wear skirts

- Men would look stupid in them
- You can see their legs better
- You can't wear sheer fishnet stockings with casual slacks

- It's not so much fun slowly sliding your hand up someone's jeans
- You could superglue a pound coin to the pavement just outside Top Shop and get an afternoon of cheap thrills
- Because they should never wear the trousers in any relationship
- Because it doesn't have quite the same ring to say you're out to 'Pull a bit of trouser' tonight

FAT PEOPLE — places they shouldn't be allowed

- In fully laden airliners
- Cake shops
- Anywhere decent people are trying to eat
- On your sofa
- Nudist colonies
- Fire exits
- On your roof
- On your lap
- On the other end of a see-saw to a midget with a precarious grip on the handle

FAT — why it's not a feminist issue

- It's caused by an accumulation of fatty deposits in the body, not Marxist-Leninist-Base-Superstructure-Gender-Adherence issues
- Stuffing your face with sticky buns has nothing to do with contemporary women's issues — and everything to do with being a pig
- Men get fat too — and that's nothing to do with feminism
- It's trendy to be thin — and why should we be forced to go against fashion by some hysterical rebels?
- It's all very well not caring that you're fat, but try buying decent clothes . . .
- Wanting to look dead tasty instead of consuming

64

something dead tasty is not a betrayal of sisterhood
- It's up to a bloke if he wants to go out with a fat bird or not

FEMALES — some useful politically incorrect terms to call them

- Girls
- Birds
- Chicks
- Bits of skirt
- Bits of fluff
- Girlies
- Wenches
- Bimbos
- Tarts
- Luv
- Darlin'
- Bints
- Babes
- Dollface
- Broads
- Floozies

FEMINISTS — 10 ways to spot one

- They say 'no' when you try to get a snog off them
- They behave like 'one of the lads'
- They look like 'one of the lads'
- They always have a crumpled Virago paperback in their handbag
- And they hit you if you ask if it's a Mills & Boon
- They're smarter than you are
- They think they're too good for you
- They insist on paying their share of a date — just so they don't feel obliged to shag you
- They don't laugh at your favourite jokes
- They do laugh at your favourite chat-up routines

FILMS — how classic feature films may have to be retitled to appease 'the politically correct brigade'

- *Vertically Challenged, Vertically Enhanced Person of Male Gender* — starring Dustin Hoffman (*Little Big Man*)

- *Jurassic Non-mammalian Exploitation Centre* — by Steven Spielberg (*Jurassic Park*)
- *Gravitationally Challenged* — starring Michael Douglas (*Falling Down*)
- *Life-inconveniencing Heterosexualist Role-playing* — starring Michael Douglas and Glenn Close (*Fatal Attraction*)
- *The Corporeal-Depriver* — starring Arnold Schwarzenegger (*The Terminator*)
- *The Corporeal-Depriver 2* — starring Arnold Schwarzenegger (*Terminator 2*)
- *Pre-Adult, DNA-Challenged, Non-Mammalian Animals Possessed of Positive Violence Skills* — starring four berks in costumes (*Teenage Mutant Ninja Turtles*)
- *The Greatest Public Control and Pacification Programme Ever Devised* — starring Charlton Heston as Moses (*The Greatest Story Ever Told*)
- *Emanuelle Participates in a Mutually Acceptable and Negotiated Marriage Partner Exchange Programme* — starring no one in particular (*Emmanuelle Meets the Wife Swappers*)

FIREARMS — why every policeman should carry one

- Virtually every crook carries one
- Bullets cost pennies — court cases can cost millions
- Fewer cases would come to court and the prison population would be severely reduced accordingly
- It's easy for a smart lawyer to get a scrote off a charge — it's not so easy to get him off a slab
- There'd soon be far more council flats available for the homeless and needy

FISHING — why it doesn't count as a blood sport

- It's too popular
- Fish can't scream
- We know that fish don't have any feelings. We've asked them
- Lots of people throw them back in again afterwards, with nothing more than a slightly cut lip
- You never hear of 'fish saboteurs'
- Most fish are slowly dying from the water pollution anyway, so you're doing them a kindness by putting them out of their misery
- Fish thrash around when you land them because they don't have legs, not because they're slowly suffocating
- Fish aren't really animals, they're — fish
- They don't bleed much

FLATULENCE — why it's good and politically incorrect to fart a lot

- The methane gas released helps to break down the ozone layer
- It puts posh people off their dinner in swish restaurants
- You can 'aromatically invade' the living space of another, as a politically correct person might complain
- Natural bodily functions are nothing to be ashamed of; you should be free to fart, lust and fight, as it's your birthright
- It's a way of telling the boss that you don't really care what he thinks during a frank and open discussion
- According to chaos theory, one fart can alter the whole world's weather pattern — and hopefully your ripper will eventually turn into a cyclone which devours half of Kansas

- It introduces a note of quiet (or not so quiet) contempt on a date which many women take to be a challenge . . .
- It is a good way of showing political discontent to any politician present, especially if you drop your trousers at the same time

FOLLICLE CLEANSING — why ginger-headed people need to be forced out of our society

- They're bad-tempered — probably because they have ginger hair
- They lower property values when they move into an area
- They have complexions like cheese and tomato pizzas
- Their hair often resembles an explosion in a Lucozade factory
- They have ginger nose hairs, often in abundance
- They have red pubic hair — which is too revolting to even think about (so forget we ever mentioned it)
- Everywhere you go, they stick out like a sore thumb, making you feel there's more of them than us
- They are bare-faced liars. They call themselves redheads. Since when has orange been red?
- Fergie has ginger hair . . .

FOLK WISDOM — phrases which prove just what a lot of bollocks it really is

- Smile and the world smiles with you
- Tomorrow is another day
- Schooldays are the happiest days of your life
- Two can live as cheapily as one. (In reality two can live as expensively as one)
- When I was your age . . . (followed by anything)

- When the going gets tough, the tough get going. (No they don't, they have massive cardiacs)
- The secret of success is hard work
- There's no such thing as a free ride. (Oh yes? Let's all ring up Prince Edward and ask him, shall we?)
- Money isn't everything
- You can't buy happiness
- Looks don't matter
- You can never be too rich or too thin. (Perhaps someone ought to ask Karen Carpenter about that; anyone got an ouija board?)
- Crime doesn't pay

FOOD — some euphemisms for what it really is

- Rump steak — cow's bum
- Veal — slaughtered baby calf that's been kept in the worst conditions imaginable since the day it was born
- Lobster Thermidor — a lobster that's been cooked alive
- Shoulder of mutton — armpit of sheep
- Pork sausage — virtually everything else you can name except pork
- Black pudding — assorted guts, blood and intestines
- Halal meat — a cow that's been strung upside down, had its throat cut and left to bleed to death
- Roast chicken — more properly 'scalded-to-death chicken', since it's estimated that up to 27 million chickens a year are still alive and conscious when plunged upside down into the scald tank at the end of the slaughter belt
- Mortadella — dead donkey
- Pork scratchings — you *really* don't want to know this one

FOOD ADDITIVES — why we should be pressing for more

- Anything that can bring a bit of colour to our otherwise bland dinner table should be welcomed
- Children love staying up until 2 a.m., jumping up and down on the sofa with a glazed expression
- You'll wonder how you ever survived until the invention of lemonade with a shelf-life of 18 years
- Reading the E-numbers on a label is an interesting way to relieve the monotony in a supermarket
- Monosodium glutamate never killed anyone
- It gives scientists a good grounding before they go to work for Dulux

FOREIGN LANGUAGES — why we shouldn't bother to learn them

- Everybody speaks English anyway
- If people like the Chinese or Russians want us to speak their language, they should at least have the decency to use the same alphabet as us
- As long as you know the local lingo for 'Fancy a shag?', you'll always get by
- Any good film or pop song is in English anyway
- Most foreign languages sound stupid
- Most foreign languages are stupid
- It really, really pisses off the French — which is a good enough reason in itself
- If you told people you were bi-lingual, most of them would shy away from you
- Two fingers pretty much covers everything you'd ever want to say to a foreigner anyway

FOX-HUNTING — why it must continue

- We mustn't give in to the masses
- It's ripping fun
- The fox population would get out of control and, by the year 2000, we'd be up to our necks in fox pooh
- It's illegal to hunt plebs
- It gives secure employment to country oafs, low-born sycophants and natural sadists who couldn't get jobs anywhere else
- The landed gentry would be at a loose end if hunting was banned — and God only knows what they'd come up with as an alternative
- It's a great British tradition — like witch ducking and racially motivated murders

FREAK SHOWS — why they should be brought back

- Kids today don't know what real entertainment is
- Freakshows are no more degrading than *Stars in Their Eyes*
- Bearded ladies should be behind bars, not behind the perfume counter of Debenhams
- Where else could you ever hope to meet someone who's half-man, half-slug (except running a firm of accountants)
- Not allowing freakshows discriminates against geeks, pencilnecks and other assorted unfortunates who were guaranteed secure employment in the honoured 'freak' profession

FREEMASONRY IN THE POLICE — why it's a good thing

- It ensures that everybody in charge is pulling in the same direction

- Anything that can get you off drink-driving offences must be worth joining
- It's one of the only chances they get to learn a funny handshake outside the Boy Scouts
- The threat of having their tongue torn out by the root and buried in the sand at low-water mark teaches officers the importance of keeping a secret
- Apart from barbecues, they rarely get the opportunity to wear an apron
- It enables officers to have close ties with local businessmen or councillors, thus strengthening community relationships

FRENCH — some choice words/phrases to upset them

- Horatio Nelson
- Retreat from Moscow
- Franco–Prussian War
- Waterloo
- Vichy Government
- Agincourt
- General de Gaulle's nose
- Greenpeace protestors in New Zealand
- Algeria

FRENCH NUCLEAR TESTING IN THE PACIFIC — why it should continue

- It keeps the water nice and warm
- If they don't test the weapons, how can they be sure they'll work?
- It's awkward to test them in France
- Or Belgium, much as they'd like to
- The fish don't seem to object
- It gives Greenpeace a chance to try out their rubber dinghies
- One day they might get lucky and hit Japan

FUR COATS — why wearing them should be positively encouraged

- They're sexier than anoraks
- They give minks a purpose in life
- Hollywood starlets would look silly wearing plastic macs
- It keeps endangered species on their toes
- Coats made from animals' teeth or tongues would look silly
- They keep you nice and warm

GANDHI — why the British Government didn't respect him as a figure of any political importance

- It's difficult to respect any statesman who wears sandals
- Or dirty bed linen
- Or who was nicknamed 'Randy'
- He looked like that little bald man in Benny Hill
- He drank his own urine (true)
- And roller-skated to work (untrue)
- You couldn't bribe him (unlike any other political leader in the world)
- He trained as a solicitor (and who respects them?)

GERMANS — why it's perfectly acceptable to hate their guts

- They started World War One
- They started World War Two
- They're probably going to start World War Three
- They're all fat and miserable and ugly but think they're the master race

- Their language is as ugly as they are
- They think *Lederhosen* are socially acceptable
- They're just dying to put on the black leather jackboots again, you know they are
- The authorities say they are trying to crush the neo-Nazis — by restricting immigration. Oh, what a giveaway . . .
- They do thigh-slapping dances and think that makes them jolly, likeable fellows
- Ironically, they themselves have escaped remarkably lightly from racial abuse with terms like 'hun', 'Fritz', 'kraut' and 'sausage eater'. Hardly cutting and wounding, are they?
- They're going to run Federal Europe one day. Now put down this book and go to sleep if you can . . .

GHETTOS — why they're good places to live

- They're one of the few places that have any real community spirit
- Everyone living there has something in common
- Political and social unrest has got to start somewhere
- They inspired that great 1969 Elvis Presley hit
- Without them we wouldn't have had a word for a huge, portable cassette player
- There are not many places where you can hang out on fire escapes
- Or hear the latest Ice Cube album played at 430 decibels at 4 a.m.
- The large presence of police cars should keep the crime rate down
- It's fun to experience the camaraderie of gang life

GIANT PANDAS — why it doesn't matter if they become extinct

- What's one less furry species in the world?
- They're always hiding in their little house when you go to the zoo so no one will miss them
- We don't rely on them for food
- There are plenty of other animals we can kill for their fur
- There'll be more bamboo shoots available for Chinese restaurants
- Governments will be able to stop wasting money flying them from zoo to zoo to see if they'll get their leg over with foreign pandas
- The dodo and the moa became extinct and that's no big deal
- Ditto the stegosaurus
- Anyone with a name like 'Ching-Ching' or 'Bing-Bing' or 'Ling-Ling' deserves extinction

GIRLIE MAGS — why women like appearing in them

- They feel they're doing something worthwhile in the name of art
- It could be their big break if they're spotted by the casting director of a porno film
- They can put 'international glamour model' on their CV
- It's difficult to find any other sort of job when your bra size equals your IQ
- They love reading the witty captions next to the photos (or having them read out to them)

GLOBAL VILLAGE — one idea in which the politically correct are right — and here's why . . .

- The Australians are the village idiots
- The Japanese are the family that keep themselves to themselves

- Turkey is the silage heap
- The Americans are the rich new family who have moved in and ruined the old manor house with lots of tacky facia work
- Wales is the horsedroppings you find outside your door in the morning
- The Germans are the family who keep their curtains drawn, but from whose house you occasionally hear screaming at night
- The French are the family next door with whom you're locked in a perpetual squabble
- Israel are the squatters at No. 23
- The English are the rough country bumpkin family everyone else looks down on
- The Third World is the council housing estate planned on the edge of the village which all the villagers are fighting to prevent

GOD — why there isn't a Mrs God

- Would you stick with a lazy good-for-nothing who does bugger-all all day?
- Perhaps God is gay
- Or divorced
- Maybe He hasn't met the right deity yet
- He enjoys playing the field, as Mary found to her cost
- Women are too scared to ask Him out for a date
- He's shy (He certainly hides himself away pretty well . . .)
- He's waiting for Kim Basinger to die
- There are no women of his age around and He doesn't want to be seen as a cradle-snatcher
- If God is the size of the universe no woman in her right mind would want to iron His shirts (and if she did, she'd need an iron the size of the Milky Way)

GOLDFISH — why it's good for funfairs to give them away as prizes

- Something requiring skills as special as hitting a playing card with darts deserves an exceptional prize
- Funfairs would lose money if they gave away tropical fish as prizes
- It teaches children about caring for pets
- And also about the transience of life
- It's better than winning a puppy in a plastic bag full of water
- You don't need to pay for medical insurance or get the vet to give them jabs
- You soon become an expert in fin rot
- Your cat can enjoy a treat after a few desperate hours

GORILLAS — why we wouldn't miss them if they became extinct tomorrow

- When was the last time you actually *needed* a gorilla?
- It's not as if they're close friends or anything
- There'd be all the more bananas for us
- Because they mostly live in Rwanda and how likely are you ever to go there?
- A walking rug that smells like a toilet is no great loss to the ecosystem
- We've got all the film we need of them to know what they once looked like
- Their only contribution to world culture has been *King Kong* and *Planet of the Apes*
- We'd still have plumbers and builders

GRANNY — 10 sure signs that it's time to dump her in a home

- She comes down the stairs stark naked and asks if you're Cousin Norman

- She goes out shopping and comes back with a snooker table and two yoghurts
- She starts to mistake the oven for her commode
- She can no longer tell the difference between a Polo mint and a used cornplaster
- She tells you she's been picked for the British Downhill Bobsleigh team and asks if she can practise by sliding down the stairs on your tea tray
- She laughs all the way through *News at Ten*
- She laughs all the way through *The Bobby Davro Show*
- She says 'hello' to you in the morning — 1,100 times in slow succession
- You take her to see your GP and he starts making 'loony' signs at you behind her back
- Her savings have run out and she costs more to keep than her pension brings in

THE GREENHOUSE EFFECT — why it's good news for Britain

- It'll be nice and warm
- We'll all be sexy and suave like Italians, riding around on Vespas all day long and pinching girls' bums

THE GREEN PARTY — why you must never, ever vote for them

- They'll confiscate our cars and give us all tricycles with Noddy bells on them
- They'll increase taxes to give social security benefits to trees and shrubs
- The next leader of their party could well be a vole
- Their idea of a defence strategy is a line of Venus flytraps along the South Coast
- It will be illegal *not* to make your own pottery

- All the council tower blocks will have to have thatched roofs
- All industry will shut down and you'll spend the rest of your days working a Spinning Jenny or weaving baskets
- The Houses of Parliament will be moved to Kew Gardens and a 'sitting' will become an al fresco vegetarian picnic-cum-discussion workshop
- Half the country's gross national product will be spent on building a giant special protection area for newts
- There will be equal rights for carrots

GULF WAR — why it was brilliant

- It's not every day you get the chance to see a laser-guided missile destroy a bridge
- It enabled thousands of journalists in the Middle East to fiddle their expenses
- It pissed off the pacifists
- It made paying taxes to fund an army and airforce worthwhile
- It made you proud to be British (a rare opportunity)
- We may be crap at football but when it comes to low-level precision bombing . . .
- No bombs got dropped on Britain
- Due to our technical expertise and advanced weaponry we managed to keep Iraqi civilian casualties down to just tens of thousands
- We won

GUNS — why they're good

- They're a great comfort if you're sexually inadequate
- They give you an excuse to wear T-shirts saying 'Kill 'em all. Let God sort them out'

- Lee Harvey Oswald got his come-uppance with a gun
- They make law enforcement far more exciting
- They're far easier to conceal than crossbows
- You can play Russian roulette when you're pissed
- You can shoot people you don't like
- You can shoot people you do like
- You can shoot people you don't know
- They're a great equaliser (unless you've got a .38 and they've got a chain-gun stolen from an Apache Gunship)

HAMPSTEAD — things we could do to it, just for the hell of it

- Build a massive complex on Hampstead Heath to house all the problem families in Britain that Hampsteadites are always defending
- Close down all the exclusive bars and boutiques and replace them with the world's biggest branch of Woolworth's
- Make it illegal for any local cinema to show anything other than *Death Wish* and *Death Wish II*
- Make it a criminal offence to be caught in possession of muesli
- Make each household take in a homeless person (then we'd see how liberal they really are)
- Make it illegal to be fat, rich, pompous, arrogant, successful or a media personality within a five-mile radius
- Convert Hampstead Ponds into the world's largest outdoor urine storage tanks

HARI-KIRI — why the Japanese commit ritual suicide

- Because they're bonkers
- So would you if you were Japanese
- So would you if you worked 23 hours a day
- It's no fun being five feet tall
- Because there are no vacancies for Kamikazes any more
- They are a humble people — and feel disgraced by their own success
- They have been caught out buying a foreign product
- Every single cinema in Tokyo shows nothing but *Godzilla* movies
- Because there isn't a dolphin around to cut up instead
- Because they should

HARMONY — how we can bring people of differing races and religions together in peace and harmony

- Straight-jacketed and gagged
- By holding their children as hostages during the encounter
- At gunpoint
- With copious amounts of mind-altering drugs
- With a heavy police presence
- With threats of truly terrible reprisals if they're not nice to each other
- Bribe them with incredibly huge amounts of non-taxable cash
- By isolating and shooting all the bastards within each group prior to the encounter
- By education (that's the biggest joke in the whole book)

'HEALTH NAZIS' — how to spot one

- They actually take your cigarette out of your mouth while you're smoking it and stamp it out
- If they see you with a can of diet cola, you're in for a 20-minute lecture on Nutrasweet
- They're running about in jogging pants even before the sound of the milkfloat in the mornings
- If you offer them an alcoholic beverage of any sort, they'll slap your face
- They offer to draw up the world's most revolting diet sheet if you're an ounce overweight
- They talk about 'going for the burn' and actively criticise you for not running a marathon a day
- They're the only ones in the entire restaurant drinking carrot juice and eating a plate of broccoli
- They have the kind of glazed, zealous look you normally associate with psychopaths or born-again Christians
- They drop dead in their mid-thirties and you all have a big laugh about it

HITLER — reasons why our Adolf wasn't such a bad person after all

- He made Winston Churchill look positively handsome and virile by comparison
- He proved to the world that having only one testicle need not be a debilitating political drawback, allowing people like Jacques Delors to have a future
- He proved to the world that being ugly and brutal-looking need not be a debilitating political drawback, allowing people like Norman Tebbit to have a future
- He made the ugly little toothbrush moustache

go out of fashion for ever. (If he'd only had the sense to dress the Gestapo in flares and tank tops, we could have been spared the 1970s as well ...)

- He made friends with club-footed little gimps like Goebbels and fat transvestite junkies like Goering when perhaps more liberal people might have shunned them
- He was a *vegetarian* (so much for them being better than the rest of us)
- It was thanks to him that John Cleese was able to do that cracking *Fawlty Towers* episode about the Germans ('Don't mention the war ...')
- He was fifty years ahead of his time in dreaming of a united Europe
- He shot himself

HOSPITALS — why more should be closed

- The staff are so inept these days, you stand a better chance of surviving by taking two aspirin and staying at home
- You can't get into one as it is
- It would challenge lazy Mills & Boon writers to think of more original characters and settings
- Nurses would be better off on the dole
- If you found yourself in a bed in a shut-down hospital, you'd probably *increase* your chances of seeing a physician
- Have you ever tasted hospital 'food'?
- You'd be less inclined to drink and drive if you knew that the nearest A&E was 360 miles away
- It would reduce the waiting list for operations like hip replacements — because you can't have a waiting list for a place that's been shut down

HUMAN SACRIFICE — why it should be brought back

- According to Politically Correct thinking, we are supposed to respect other people's customs and values
- Sometimes only a dead gameshow host can appease the gods (apparently)
- Tearing the still-beating heart out of a painter and decorator might not appease the wrath of the gods, but think of the satisfaction . . .
- The still-beating heart could then be used as a donor organ for a more valuable member of society — like a peeping Tom
- God doesn't seem to respond to prayers any more, so perhaps human sacrifice is worth a go . . .
- It could get terrific TV ratings, with a commentary by Saint and Greavsie as the ceremony progresses
- Liberal do-gooders would volunteer to be sacrificed in droves 'for the good of the community' — and we'd soon be shot of the lot of them
- Tossing people from Essex into the water as an act of appeasement to the river god Thames might prevent London from flooding. (If not, there's always the Thames barrier, so we're covered either way)
- We could think of it as a form of 'community service' for criminals

HUNGER — why we shouldn't send food to the starving nations

- Do they ever send us food?
- We don't know their full postal address
- One day you'll be dying for a cheese and pickle

sandwich, only to find all the cheese has gone abroad
- Everyone knows that the food never reaches the starving — the local government nicks it all and scoffs it
- People must understand that, in life, there's no such thing as a free lunch
- A packet of Bourbon biscuits in a cardboard tube marked 'urgent' isn't going to help very much
- If we wait long enough, the Americans or some other bunch of UN troops will kill them all in 'friendly fire' incidents
- The EC won't donate its food mountains — and they must have a good reason for that, mustn't they?

HUNT SABOTEURS — why they're scum

- They dress so grubbily compared to the nice smart huntsmen
- Many of them are students — or *vegetarians*
- Or both
- These people have no respect for their social betters
- They make respectable country towns look untidy with their filthy little vans
- Dissent is what made Britain great — which is why it is heroic for the huntsmen to refuse to bow to pressure and intimidation
- They spoil all the fun that the fox derives from the thrill of the hunt
- By leaving false trails with scented rags, they leave the countryside smelling like a tart's boudoir
- They tend to fall under the wheels of horseboxes or Land Rovers, getting injured and thereby wasting NHS resources
- They attack huntsmen's whips with their faces, sometimes snapping them

THE HUSBAND'S CHARTER — things married men should be automatically entitled to

- Ironed shirts
- Clean underwear
- A spick and span house
- Dinner on the table
- Sex on demand
- The right to watch soccer whenever it's on TV
- A discreet bit on the side
- To let themselves go once married, giving up all pretence of both a waistline and a hairline
- The wife to keep herself just as tasty as she was when they got married
- The right to quit all that 'romantic' shit they had to come up with to get her to the altar

INCONTINENT PEOPLE — records to wind them up

- *Here I Go Again*
- *Rainy Night in Georgia*
- *Go Now*
- *Can't Keep It In*
- *Waterloo*
- *Born to Run*
- *We(e) are the World*
- *Desperado*
- Anything by Wet, Wet, Wet
- Anything by the Go Go's

INDIAN RESTAURANTS — how to have the perfect politically incorrect evening in one

- 11.08 Discuss the choice of restaurant
- 11.09 Refreshments are served
- 11.17 Burp the top ten dance chart
- 11.24 Start of the grand 'Down Your Pint in One' contest
- 11.32 'Poppadom Frisbee' competition

- 11.33 Commence sexual harassment of two girls sitting opposite
- 11.58 First fight of the evening (always a momentous occasion)
- 12.07 Start of the 'Pilau Rice Flicking' contest
- 12.16 Second fight of the evening (something of an anti-climax, this one)
- 12.24 Start of the 'See Who's the Most Flatulent' contest (continues throughout remainder of the evening)
- 12.39 Synchronised regurgitating
- 12.45 The arrival of the bill (preceding, as it does, the act commonly known as 'Doing a runner')
- 01.15 The arrival of the Old Bill (too late, as usual)

INTEREST RATE — why it should be kept high

- It encourages people to save
- It means that people with loads of savings can make lots of money
- It teaches a lesson to those people who bought bigger houses than they needed
- It's a good incentive to make sure you pay off your Barclaycard bill each month
- It encourages people to work harder so they won't lose their job and have to give up their home
- It encourages the repossession of homes, therefore putting more houses on the market and reducing prices
- It teaches people to live within their means
- It keeps the bailiffs busy
- A big house becomes even more of a status symbol
- It will precipitate a General Election

INTERMARRIAGE — why it's good to marry your sister

- When your parents come to visit they can see both their children at the same time
- Your wife won't have to change her name
- You'll have first-hand knowledge of her family background
- You'll know all her previous boyfriends
- You'll save on birthday presents because your mother and mother-in-law will be one and the same person
- You can invite both your parents to dinner and you'll only have to cook for four people!
- It makes it easier to remember your wife's birthday
- You can save money because you only have to invite one set of guests to your wedding
- Your children will have three heads and you can sell them to the circus

INTERNATIONAL ARMS DEALER — why it's more fun than being a biscuit salesman

- Imagine the commission on selling just one aircraft carrier — you'd have to sell 1,000,000,000,000,000,000,000,000,000,000,000,000 packets of Jaffa Cakes to even come close
- When friends ask you what you do for a living you can mysteriously wink and tap your nose instead of saying, 'I'm divisional sales manager for Huntley & Palmers'
- You get to travel the world, instead of the corner shops of Salford
- You can put things like 'assassination of international supergrass' down on your expenses sheet
- It's much more exciting to demonstrate a Dart surface-to-air missile than it is a Garibaldi

- By and large, it is easier to sell mortars to the Mujahadeen than Jacobs Crackers
- Biscuits go mouldy; hand grenades don't, so your car stock has a longer life
- Wafers are not a high status product in the Third World — AK47s are
- You can always expand into high profit areas like nerve gas; in the 'biscuit game', all you can hope for is to shift a few Christmas selection tins

INTERNATIONAL CURRENCY SPECULATION — why it's fun

- You can make billions just by tapping a few numbers on your PC
- If some foreign scum football team beat England last night (which is likely), you can wreck their national currency in revenge
- You know that you're more powerful than any elected government
- Most of the time, you're playing with other people's money, so if you fuck up it doesn't matter
- If you dislike a particular company, you can invest their entire pension plan funds in the El Salvadorian Colon, secure in the knowledge that, within 25 minutes, it won't even pay for a round of cheese sandwiches off the tea trolley
- You can play fun games like 'Start the Trend'. This involves suddenly and mysteriously investing all your money in an obscure African currency like the Nigerian Kobo. All the other speculators, thinking you know something they don't, will rush to follow suit. The currency will rise in value — and you get out quick with the profits before everyone else realises they've been suckered. Other fun games include 'Wreck the ERM' and 'Put the Shits up the Bundesbank'

- If you want to buy a holiday home in the Dordogne (like, you're a completely boring bastard or something), you can take all your money out of francs, thus causing the currency to nosedive and enabling you to buy your property at a relatively cheaper rate. This also applies when you run out of Perrier
- With enough capital behind you, you can hold entire governments to ransom. You can phone up Clinton at the White House and say, 'Bill, if your wife isn't here giving me a blow job within the hour, the dollar is going to slide five cents against the deutschmark ... capish?'
- If your wife's giving you a hard time, you can take it out on the economies of entire continents

IVORY POACHING — why elephants could do without tusks

- They always get in the way when they French kiss
- An overbite is *never* attractive
- Basketball matches between two elephant teams would last longer than six seconds
- They wouldn't snag pullovers every time they wore them
- Or take another elephant's eye out during a rugby scrum
- Or cause havoc when they attempted to get through a revolving door
- They wouldn't always be asked to do their plate-spinning trick at jungle parties
- Think of the toothpaste they'd save
- They wouldn't get shot

JAPANESE COMPANIES — how to be politically incorrect if you work for one

- Challenge the management to a basketball match. (They're all short and don't stand a hope)
- Phone up the MD anonymously and tip him off that the war crimes commission are investigating him
- Suggest that your annual works outing should be an Orient Express type journey . . . in Burma
- Celebrate the anniversary of the bombing of Hiroshima by running around the factory floor with your arms outstretched going 'Waaaaaaaaaaaaaaaaaaa! KABOOOOOOOOOOOOO MMMMM!'
- Ensure all the dishes served in the canteen contain mushrooms (the Japanese are strangely upset by this shape)
- Make sure that the company film society holds regular screenings of *Midway*, *The Sands of Iwo Jima*, *Tora! Tora! Tora!*, *Bridge over the River Kwai* and *Hiroshima Mon Amour*
- Wear a 'Save the Whale' T-shirt to work

JESUS — why you should give yourself over to him completely

- You can't cope with real life
- You've stopped taking your medication
- Worshipping Noddy didn't work, so maybe He's worth a try
- Everybody else hates you
- He comes to you at night dressed like the blonde girl from Abba
- He died for your sins — all you got was a six-month suspended sentence
- It's better than giving yourself over to Peter Purves — who didn't want you anyway
- Two nice young men with big big smiles and unblinking eyes visited your house and told you what He has to offer

JOBS — politically incorrect career choices

- Lumberjack
- The person who cuts off the electricity supply in old people's houses
- Freelance seal culler
- Estate agent
- Bailiff
- Psychopathic axe murderer
- Editor of the *Sun*
- Captain of a whaler
- Butcher
- Professional wheel clamper

JOB ADVERTISEMENTS — some politically incorrect words and phrases to use

- Special consideration will be given to applicants who are double-jointed and who go like the clappers
- A company car is provided but you are expected to use only the back seat

- Perks include use of the MD's love nest
- This post is not open to candidates with boyfriends over 5 feet 6 inches tall
- Fluency in talking dirty is an advantage
- Candidates must be used to working without supervision (or clothing)
- Applicants must be educated to at least A-level standard, preferably at schools with high levels of discipline where they might have got a taste for a good caning
- Duties include filing, word processing, photocopying and smearing raspberry jam all over your immediate boss before licking it off
- Some experience in sleeping your way to the top is preferable, though not essential

KERB CRAWLING — why it's a really good idea

- It's much more convenient than having to stop your car, get out and personally go up to every single woman you fancy
- Women love the attention
- It enables you to practise slow driving techniques, including advanced clutch control
- If you've got a flash car it gives you the chance to show it off to maximum effect
- If you do have an accident caused by taking your eyes off the road, driving at slow speeds means you're much less likely to be injured
- Because you're driving so slowly, women are much more likely to be able to hear your lewd suggestions
  - It's a very fuel-efficient way of motoring
- There's no danger of being stopped for speeding
- Judges, Justices of the Peace and ex-DPPs do it all the time

MARTIN LUTHER KING — 10 things he was crap at

- Darts
- Remembering his mother's birthday

- Hitting the manufacturer's tradename on the back of a urinal
- Inspiring a hit musical based on his life
- Long division
- Doing impressions of Smokey Robinson and the Miracles
- Guessing who did it in Cluedo
- Winning *two* Nobel Peace prizes
- Knowing when he'd said too much
- Ducking

KINGS — nicknames that Prince Charles is likely to have when he becomes the monarch

- Charles the Old
- Charles the Very Old
- Charles the Senile and Decrepit
- Charles the Big-Eared
- Charles the Bald
- Charles the Ugly
- Charles the Animal Butcher
- Charles the Last

KU-KLUX-KLAN — everything you require to start your own local branch

- Five members all called 'Bubba'
- Two members who are sleeping with their sisters
- Two other members who are married to their sisters
- Lots of balding old men with rippling double chins who represent the Aryan Super-race
- A large wooden cross and some petrol
- A nod and a wink from the local lawman
- A collection of Kenny Rogers albums
- A shell-shocked veteran who'll do anything — which is useful considering how chickenshit the rest of the members are likely to be
- A black person, preferably small, elderly and on their own

LABORATORY RATS — reasons for their continued use

- Laboratory rabbits or beagles wouldn't be able to fit into those tiny little mazes
- If you need to cut the tail off something as part of an experiment they're ideally suited
- Because they're not cuddly you don't get the public outcry against using them
- They're cheap
- They can't say no
- They're easy to flush down the toilet afterwards
- Unlike dogs, cats, bunnies etc., there are no cuddly rats in children's books or TV (Splinter from Teenage Mutant Ninja Turtles doesn't count; neither does that washed-up has-been Roland Rat)

THE LAST SUPPER — politically incorrect things one of the disciples could have said on the night of our Lord's greatest tribulation

- 'Where's all the crumpet, Jesus?'
- 'Go on, Jesus, you're first for the Karaoke tonight!'
- 'Look, I only had juice, so I don't see why I should pay towards the wine . . .'
- 'Hang on, the Strip-o-Gram should be here in about five minutes'
- 'You hit the nail right on the head there, mate . . .'
- 'Cheer up, Jeezy mate, it may never happen'
- 'There was this Pharisee and this donkey, right, and there's no one around, right, so the Pharisee thinks . . .'
- 'If you're planning on staying in Jerusalem, Lord, who's going to put you up?'

THE LAW — why you should take it into your own hands

- If you've ever had the police try to solve anything for you, you'll already know why and you can skip the rest of this list
- The police can only slap someone's wrist — you can crack someone's head with a baseball bat
- The police require proof — all you need is a brick and the element of surprise
- The scrote will be out on bail in a week if you let the law take its course — but he won't be back on the streets if he's six feet under your geraniums
- There's something strangely satisfying about someone who's previously done you wrong now kneeling in front of you, pleading for you not to castrate him

- The police need a search warrant — you only need a big sledgehammer
- A £30 fine is no substitute for watching the scum's home go up in flames
- Juries can be fixed — severed spinal columns can't
- Freemasons can easily escape justice — but it's harder for them to dodge a thrusting Black & Decker
- If the law can't catch a criminal, you're in with a bloody good chance of getting away with it too.

LEAD POISONING — signs that it's already taking a toll on the nation's youth

- Have you ever watched *Parallel 9* on Saturday mornings?
- They've made a new series of the *Tomorrow People*
- Rave music
- None of them realise that 1970s fashions are disgusting, not trendy
- The Territorials are up to strength
- Teenage Mutant Ninja Turtles
- It is no longer possible to stage BBC's *Top of the Form* — because no one qualifies any more
- No article in *Fast Forward* is longer than 20 words
- They enjoyed *Stingray* when it was shown again
- The top children's hero is Arnold Schwarzenegger. Need we say more?

LEARNING — why it's bad for you

- The world isn't geared to you
- Twats in their thousands say, 'You swallowed a dictionary, mush?'

- You feel alone, alienated and unable to converse with ordinary people
- You think ordinary people hate you
- Ordinary people *do* hate you
- The world doesn't want thinkers, it wants workers
- You'll be overqualified for 95 per cent of the jobs on offer
- You'll probably realise that religion makes no sense and that life is pointless and death is for ever — dilemmas that people whose lips move when they read the *Sun* page 3 captions never have to deal with
- Complete strangers want to beat you up because they've found you in possession of a book
- People stare at you if you read in a public place and ask, 'Why are you reading a book?' (Saying 'So I don't end up like you' is not recommended)
- You'll probably pass it on to your children and they'll suffer the same way you have

SPIKE LEE — proof that he's a crap director

- No one even considered inviting him to make *Terminator 2*
- You never see sequels to any of his films; any bets on *Malcolm X II*?
- No one's ever invited him to front a TV mystery-thriller series called *Spike Lee Presents* . . .
- Not one of his films has featured a top actor like Arnold Schwarzenegger or 'Sly' Stallone
- *Jungle Fever* did not feature death-dealing ninja cyborgs or axe-wielding psychopaths, which any decent director knows are vital to any popular film
- Middle-class liberals like him — the kiss of death
- There are no children's action figure toys based

on any of Spike Lee's characters in *Do the Right Thing*
- He doesn't make much use of spectacular special effects to stop you from getting bored every two minutes
- You just know he couldn't make a film of the calibre of *Basic Instinct* for toffee
- Who invented ET — Spike Lee or Steven Spielberg?

LEGAL AID — why it should be stopped

- Why should we innocent people pay the court fees of the guilty ones?
- Let the bastards pay for it out of their criminal ill-gotten gains
- Only poor people qualify for legal aid — and statistically they're the ones responsible for most crimes
- If they couldn't get free legal aid, perhaps criminals would think twice before breaking the law
- It makes solicitors' paying clients jealous and resentful
- If criminals had to pay for their solicitor's time, they'd be much more likely to plead guilty and save money
- The Libyan legal system works well enough without it

JOHN LENNON — why he was really a talentless git and *not* a genius

- He wrote crap like 'I am the eggman/I am the walrus/Goo goo ga joob'
- He stayed in bed for several days to further the cause of world peace. (Strange as it may seem, this failed to win him the Nobel Peace Prize)

- While he was alive he had no solo No. 1 hits
  (even Little Jimmy Osmond, Brian & Michael,
  the St Winifred's School Choir and Clive Dunn
  had a better musical track record than this)
- He once appeared on stage at the Albert Hall
  inside a large white bag eating chocolate cake
- He posed for a film specifically about his penis
- He said he was more popular than Jesus but *A
  Spaniard in the Works* has consistently failed
  to outsell the Bible
- He had the pick of all the best spectacles that
  money could buy — and he chose stupid-
  looking granny glasses
- He had the pick of all the tastiest birds of the
  1960s — and he married Yoko Ono. (Obviously,
  the glasses were the wrong prescription)
- He didn't write 'Mull of Kintyre' which is a
  bloody good song
- He was stupid enough to stop and sign an
  autograph for a nerd with a glazed expression
  and a big hand gun

LEPROSY — why you should never give to a leprosy charity

- It is unwise to approach a hooded figure rattling
  a collection box and chanting 'Unclean!
  Unclean!'
- They should pull themselves together and take
  themselves in hand
- Superglue, which accounts for 95 per cent of
  their total budget, is not a long-term solution
- Nor are bulldog clips, which account for the
  other 5 per cent
- Lepers are not good members of society, being
  footloose and liable to throw their hand in
  when they do find regular employment
- Many of the people you are helping are complete
  flakes

LIBRARIES — how they intend to change the titles of politically incorrect sounding fiction

- *Vertically Challenged Persons of Female Gender* — by Louisa M. Alcott (*Little Women*)
- *Domiciliary Disadvantaged in Paris and London* — by George Orwell (*Down and Out in Paris and London*)
- *The Academically Challenged* — by Fyodor Dostoevsky (*The Idiot*)
- *Return of an Indigenous Ethnic Member of the Populace* — by Thomas Hardy (*Return of the Native*)
- *Lady Chatterley's Non-Platonic Spouse Equivalent* — by D. H. Lawrence (*Lady Chatterley's Lover*)
- *The Physically Challenged Person of Notre Dame* — by Victor Hugo (*The Hunchback of Notre Dame*)
- *Person and Superperson* — by George Bernard Shaw (*Man and Superman*)
- *Of Consenting Human Sexual Power Ethics Exploration* — by W. Somerset Maugham (*Of Human Bondage*)
- *Winnie the Natural Human Waste Product* — by A. A. Milne (*Winnie the Pooh*)
- *Rosencrantz and Guildenstern are Corporeally Disadvantaged* — by Tom Stoppard (*Rosencrantz and Guildenstern are Dead*)
- *Les Emotionally Challenged* — by Victor Hugo (*Les Misèrables*)
- *A Streetcar Named Sexual Harassment* — by Tennessee Williams (*A Streetcar Named Desire*)
- *Equal Among Equals* — by Jeffrey Archer (*First Amongst Equals*)
- *Self-Aggrandisement and Racial Repression* — by Jane Austen (*Pride and Prejudice*)

- *The Culturally and Ethnocentrically Biased Account of Previous Eras Person* — by Malcolm Bradbury (*The History Man*)
- *Mein Fascist Illiterate Crap* — by Adolf Hitler (*Mein Kampf*)
- *Visually Inconvenienced in the Israeli Occupied Territories* — by Aldous Huxley (*Eyeless in Gaza*)
- *One Flew Over The Home for the Emotionally Different* — by Ken Kesey (*One Flew Over the Cuckoo's Nest*)
- *Non-Domiciliary Based Salesperson, Clothing Executive, Fascist Repressive Tool, Covert Government Representative* — by John Le Carre (*Tinker, Tailor, Soldier, Spy*)
- *Not Engaged in Interpersonal Greeting but Aquatically Distressed* — by Stevie Smith (*Not Waving But Drowning*)
- *Under an Arboreal Tract of Exploitative, Involuntarily Supplied Bovine Produce* — by Dylan Thomas (*Under Milk Wood*)
- *'Tis Pity She's a Sex-Care Provider* — by John Ford (*'Tis Pity She's a Whore*)
- *The Aquatic Non-Adult Persons* — by Charles Kingsley (*The Water Babies*)
- *The Glass Non-Human Incarceration Camp* — by Tennessee Williams (*The Glass Menagerie*)
- *Moby Male Organ of Repression* — by Herman Melville (*Moby Dick*)
- *Now* — by Charles Dickens (*Hard Times*)

LIFE SUPPORT MACHINES — politically incorrect ways to justify pulling the plug on a relative

- It costs a quid to park everytime you visit the hospital
- That personal tape from Shaking Stevens didn't

work — on the contrary, it put them deeper into
their coma
- The surgeons will 'see you all right' if they can
have the organs for a private patient
- The life assurance is ready and waiting . . .
- You couldn't stand being with them while they
were conscious, and they're even more boring
now . . .
- It's been two days — time's up surely . . .
- You've got other relatives
- You fancy a boozy wake
- You keep missing *Emmerdale Farm* because of
visiting hours
- Heads they stay on the machine, tails they check
into the 'Wooden Waldorf' . . .

LITTER — why it's a good idea to drop it

- It breaks up the monotony of the pavement
- It saves someone having to empty the bins
- It gives stray hedgehogs something to live off at
night
- It gives homeless people something to live off at
night
- You live in a lousy area, and it's in keeping with
the environment
- It's a long-standing family tradition
- It's better than dropping £10 notes
- Everyone does it — and you're terrified of being
'different'
- You're a pavement artist, expressing yourself
through discarded sweet wrappers, lolly sticks
and empty fag packets
- Taking shards of glass out of dogs' paws keeps
vets in business

LLOYD'S NAMES — why they should get all their money back

- So there'll be more money to invest in the country
- If they don't, many will be bankrupt, damaging our faith in the British economy
- If they don't, they might turn to crime or drug trafficking to make ends meet
- They were just badly advised
- They're just victims of the system
- If they're made bankrupt it will make loads of chauffeurs, gardeners and maids unemployed
- So they can pass it on to their own children and let them make ill-advised investments too
- If they don't they'll be forced to sell their Rolls-Royces, bringing more on to the market and depressing the second-hand-car market
- If they don't, they'll have to move out of their luxury homes, leaving them open to squatters and costing councils thousands of pounds to evict them
- It's tragic seeing an MP or peer of the realm suddenly faced with financial ruin

LOCAL COUNCILS — why it's good to serve your area as a local councillor

- You get great bribes
- You get to go on boozy, womanising 'friendship trips' to twin towns at the ratepayer's expense
- If you hate someone, you can compulsorily purchase their home and estimate its value at 98p
- If they manage to find a new home, you can then instruct the council to compulsorily purchase the homes either side of them and allocate them to large semi-itinerant problem families who, between them, are estimated to be responsible

108

for three-quarters of all violent crime in the borough

- You can divert heavy goods traffic up your mother-in-law's road
- You can build an eight-lane flyover straight over the top of your opponent's party headquarters — and get a great bribe from the construction company doing the job at the same time
- You can threaten your local with the withdrawal of its licence — unless you get free Scotch and scampi in a basket
- Everyone knows you're a crook — but no one can do anything about it

LONDON — why it won't resemble New York in 10 years' time

- Because it already resembles it now, homey

LOVERS — cruel and improper ways to leave them which Paul Simon never thought of . . .

- Flick the Vs, Rees
- Cut off her head, Ted
- Don't give a toss, Ross
- Fracture his nose, Rose
- Do a quick bunk, Dunk
- Run off with a boy, Roy
- Tell her she's fat, Matt
- Kick him somewhere tender, Brenda
- Show her your piles, Gyles
- Leave him in physical pain, Jane
- Be swift on your toesies, Moses
- Say you prefer a wank, Frank
- Don't give a shit, Britt
- Just say 'Yah, bye', Di
- Give him the lurgie, Fergie

M25 — reasons to widen it to 14 lanes

- To make life more difficult for hedgehogs
- To enable us to have 12 fast lanes
- It's more environmentally friendly than widening it to 16 lanes
- The people whose land is compulsorily purchased will make some money
- It will make for far more dramatic lane changes
- It will enable people to get to work faster which is better for productivity and therefore the economy
  - Three lanes could be coned off without much delay to your journey time
- As a result of a really bad car crash the helicopter ambulance will have more space to land
- You'll have much more choice if you want to dump an unwanted pet

MAD COW DISEASE — how it's manifested itself in other animals

- Daft Chicken Ailment
- Loony Goat Sickness
- Demented Pig Condition

- Deranged Duckling Disorder
- Nutty Sheep Infection
- Bonkers Horse Affliction
- Insane Goose Malaise
- Potty Hen Complaint
- Premature senility

THE MAFIA — why it's a good organisation to work for

- There aren't many multi-national organisations with openings in extortion, numbers, racketeering, drug smuggling, counterfeiting, prostitution or murder
- Most job-application forms ask you how many O levels you have, not how many hammer fights you've been in
- In most businesses you have to wait until your boss retires before promotion; in the Mafia all you have to do is wait until someone cuts his throat in a barber's chair
- Most companies' expansion plans are boring and involve steady growth through sound fiscal management — not 'whacking those muthafuckers on the East Side'
- Their Head Office is somewhere fun like Las Vegas rather than Slough Industrial Estate or Telford Business Park
- You'll never be demoted (just shot in the back of the head)
- Hitting people in the bollocks with a baseball bat is frowned upon in the world of quantity surveying whereas in the Mafia you get paid time and a half for it
- Promotion isn't a matter of who you know, it's who you kill
- You don't undercut the competition — you cut them up
- Girls are more impressed by men who say they

work for the Mafia than men who say they work for Allied Dunbar (even though they're both in the insurance racket)
- Rather than suffering from wimpy occupational hazards like Repetitive Strain Injury you'll suffer from macho complaints like exit wounds
- It's a more honourable occupation than commodity dealing

MAHOGANY (AND OTHER RARE, DIMINISHING STOCKS OF HARDWOODS) — good things to make from them

- Chopsticks
- Toothpicks
- Matches
- Those little spoons you get with ice creams in the cinema
- Or the forks you get with your fish and chips
- Tongue depressors
- Sticks to support bendy plants
- Ice-lolly sticks
- Emery boards
- Cat scratching posts

JOHN MAJOR — how he could increase his popularity

- Resign
- Shoot himself
- Put on a dress, take a massive dose of testosterone and pretend he's Mrs Thatcher

NELSON MANDELA — why he's completely out of touch with the real world after being in jail since 1964

- He can't understand why other members of the ANC look at him funny when he calls them 'daddy-o' or 'hep cats'

- He can't understand why no one wants to do the Twist with him at official functions
- Winnie had to talk him out of having a mop top like the Fab Four
- He's confused by necklace killings because he thinks they're some sort of new-fangled fiery hoola-hoop craze
- He's upset because Martin Luther King doesn't return his calls
- He's tried playing CDs, but the needle keeps skimming across them
- He can't work his video machine
- He still thinks he can bring a peaceful solution to South Africa

NELSON MANDELA — politically incorrect things to say to him

- 'We've decided to lock you up again. April Fool!'
- 'Well, your release made a big difference to peace and tranquillity in South Africa, didn't it?'
- 'Nelson Mandela? Never heard of you'
- 'I wasn't even born in 1964 when they banged you up ...'
- 'Who's the wife kidnapped today then?'
- 'I bet you'd rather have stayed in jail than come home to *her* ...'
- 'I've got a dog named Nelson; funny name for a bloke though ...'
- 'I bet you a tenner you snuff it before South Africa becomes a truly democratic state'
- 'I bet you a tenner a baby born today snuffs it before South Africa becomes a truly democratic state'
- 'Mr Mandela? I've got a parcel here for you from a Mr Terreblanche ...'

MANTRAS — phrases you'll probably end up concentrating on while meditating

- 'I bet this doesn't work'
- 'Am I missing something on TV?'
- 'My leg's gone to sleep . . .'
- 'Did I leave the grill on?'
- 'Rosanna Arquette, Rosanna Arquette, Rosanna Arquette'
- 'Shit! I forgot to get some milk!'
- 'I don't feel any different . . .'
- 'Will it ruin my trance state if I just scratch my bum a bit?'
- 'What's that dark stain on the carpet?'
- 'Sod this! I'm bored'

MARX — things committed Marxists still try to keep secret about him

- Karl Marx first took up magic as a children's party entertainer, partly to pay for his lodgings in Highgate but also to lay his hands on large helpings of chocolate fingers, sausages on sticks and trifle
- However, he soon became so proficient that he turned professional in 1847
- His greatest attempted feat of magic was, unhappily, a disaster. He announced in *The Times* that he would make Capitalism vanish but, when the time came, he found he couldn't get the sheet over it and the stunt was abandoned
- His act mixed comedy with magic, making him in many ways the Paul Daniels of his day (although there is no evidence that he wore a stupid wig)
- His catchphrase — 'You're first up against the wall when the revolution comes, missus!' — was as famous as the climax of his stage act, in

which he would go among the rich audience, take their pocket watches and items of jewellery, put them in a handkerchief, smash them as hard as he could with a hammer and then run out of the fire door

- As Marx became more involved with politics and retired from the stage, he never quite forgot his love of magic and would often end his stirring lectures with a clenched-fist salute — from which would magically appear a bunch of flowers

- *The Times* for 18 July 1864 carries a report that Marx was thrown out of the British Museum Reading Room on the previous day for 'pulling an endless stream of gaily coloured knotted handkerchiefs out of his ear'

MASTURBATION — why it should become a major Olympic sport instead of an act of deep shame

- Britain would stand an excellent chance of coming first for a change
- Our athletes wouldn't require expensive training facilities, just a dirty little cubicle and an old copy of *Double D Mega-Boobs Special*
- Sports writers could have a field day with headlines like 'Hurrah! Britain pulls it off!' and 'A stroke of genius!' — or 'Britain spurts ahead in sprint event'
- It would allow most professional athletes to combine their careers with their social lives — especially weightlifters, for whom 'pumping iron' would take on a whole new meaning.
- Seb Coe could make a spectacular comeback
- Tobacco and trainer companies wouldn't be nearly so keen to offer stars of *these* Olympics ludicrous multi-million dollar sponsorship

deals — although Kleenex might take an active interest

- Once recognised as an Olympic event, masturbation will quickly become a compulsory sport in all schools — helping to provide a healthy outlet for youthful passions. (But perhaps causing a few furrowed brows at annual parents' sports days)
- The Olympics would become so vile, no TV company would broadcast it and then we wouldn't be bored rigid with sport on every channel 24 hours a day every four years. (Maybe masturbation should be introduced into the World Cup as well . . . 'He shoots, he scores!')

MATERIALISM — why it's good

- It keeps capitalism going — if you didn't buy lots of things, everyone would be out of work
- If you have nothing, people think you're scum
- Possessions give you a personal sense of security
- Demonstrating your material wealth in public says you're a success, you're powerful and sexy as hell
- You may not care about money but the water board, the gas board, the electricity board and the local council all do
- What would we do with our lives if we didn't pursue materialistic goals?
- John Lennon wrote 'Imagine no possessions . . .', but you can bet he had a bloody good stereo
- It provides a common interest to bring lonely old men and lovely young women together
- God might look after the sparrows of the field, but He's a bit more myopic about people lacking in material sustenance

MATERNITY LEAVE — why it should be outlawed

- It discriminates against men
- And lesbians
- It makes women who can't have babies bitter and twisted (like their fallopian tubes)
- What woman in her right mind would prefer going back to work to spending time at home with her feet up?
- It's women's own fault for getting pregnant — why should they have what is, in effect, subsidised shags?
- If the mother goes back to work she'll become alienated from her child who'll grow up to resent her
- It's criminal to expect a mother to have to clear up six months' worth of paperwork when she eventually returns to work
- They don't have maternity leave in Libya and the women there don't complain

MATRIARCHAL SOCIETY — why it's a bloody good job we don't live in one

- Nations wouldn't settle disputes by wars, they'd have poxy flower-arranging contests
- Frank Bruno would still be astounding us with his hands — as World Heavyweight Fretwork Champion
- The police force would burst into criminals' homes and give them a big supportive hug to make up for the love that's obviously been lacking in their lives
- Washing-up would be an Olympic sport — as would ironing
- There'd be no international wheeling and dealing on the Stock Exchange — instead there'd be an informal coffee morning cum bring 'n' buy sale

- You'd never see snooker on TV; instead there'd be lots of programmes about babies
- The government would award medals for shopping
- All the newspapers would be out of business, as gossip travels faster than newsprint
- Chris Columbus would have discovered knitting, not America
- We'd be called 'womankind' instead of 'mankind', making us men feel inferior

MEAT — reasons why it's a good idea to eat meat

- Beef Stroganoff tastes nice
- All those female hormones they pump into cattle give you bigger breasts (this is not so wonderful if you are a male meat eater)
- Hitler didn't eat meat — and he turned into a mass murderer
- Beef and two veg is a great British institution — like the Monarchy
- If cattle farmers went out of business, the towns would be full of crazed half-wits wandering about going 'ARRR' to themselves and shooting pet dogs
- If you didn't eat meat, all the abattoir workers would have to take out their psychotic impulses on you and your family instead
- Morrissey says 'Meat is murder' — and you know he always talks crap
- Believe me, you don't want to upset the powerful farming lobby . . .
- You'll eventually develop BSE, go senile and then not have to cope with your fear of growing old and dying

MEN — why they're superior

- They can go to the toilet standing up without getting their shoes wet
- They're much better at lighting their own farts
- They can belch 'God Save the Queen'
- They can identify 38 different brands of lager just by the colour of vomit
- They're better at fighting
- They can go for several months on end without doing a domestic chore
- They're more likely to have been a bully at school
- They can spit further
- They're far better at chatting up women

MEN — how to gradually increase your sexual harassment skills

- NORMAL GREETING:
Good morning, Miss Parker

- FLIRTING:
Good morning, Miss Parker. That's a lovely blouse you're wearing

- SEXISM:
Whorrr! That blouse is a bit tight, eh, darlin'?

- SEXUAL HARASSMENT:
Spread 'em or you're fired!

MENTALLY ILL PEOPLE — why the government was right to release them into the community

- We need to make savage and painful cuts somewhere — unfortunately, so do most of the people released
- If patients do a forward somersault under the

119

fast Amersham train, they won't need expensive medication any more
- No politician lives within 100 miles of any short-term hostel for the mentally ill
- It needs all the votes it can get at the next election

MICHELANGELO — why he was an arsehole

- It took him over four years to paint the ceiling of the Sistine Chapel when he could have Artexed it in a day

THE MIDDLE CLASSES — the things they do which show what prats they are

- Play each other at squash once a week and sulk for days if they lose
- Eat muesli — even though they know it tastes like nut bogie crunch with extra scabs
- Buy a big house in a slum area and say they're living a genuine multi-cultural lifestyle
- Preach about the environment and then drive around in bloody big BMWs
- Give themselves coronaries by working 20 hours a day to reach the exalted post of under-deputy manager for the stationery cupboard
- Reach for the Valium as soon as the dishwasher breaks down
- Buy a second home in Provence, which is about as exciting as Middlesbrough on a wet Sunday
- Read *The Sunday Times*
- Believe what they read in *The Sunday Times*

THE MIDDLE CLASSES — why they should be wiped off the face of the earth

- They think they can appreciate opera
- They know how to use chopsticks

- They call their children stupid names, like Jocasta or Rebecca
- They wear ties to work
- They have 'dinner parties'
- They try to do their bit for the community — like becoming Tory councillors
- They spawned Kenneth Branagh and Emma Thompson
- They make those tacky little 'quote marks' with their fingers
- They use words like *soupçon*

MIME — why it's crap

- It discriminates against the visually impaired
- When you've seen one person 'exploring a wall' you've seen them all
- Ditto 'walking in the wind'
- While you're watching them in a shopping precinct someone is stealing your wallet
- They're following in Charlie Chaplin's footsteps and he was crap, too
- If it was valid as an art form there'd be loads of world-famous mime artists instead of just one
- What's the point of pretending to be a robot?
- Even mime artists think that mime is crap — they just won't come out and say it

MINIMUM WAGE — why there should never be one

- If people are willing to work for 80p an hour, let them
- If they don't like it they can always get a better paid job elsewhere
- If you fire someone and have to give them three months' money you'll probably be able to do it out of the small change in your pocket

121

- In these difficult times you've got to reduce your overheads somehow
- You can give employees a 100 per cent pay rise and hardly notice your increased payroll
- It lets workers avoid paying income tax
- It will make Britain more competitive in the international market
- It stops employees from wasting money on booze and cigarettes
- If workers have to contribute one per cent of their income to a pension fund they'll hardly notice it

MISS WORLD — why the championship was such a good idea

- It was a rare chance to see exquisite beauties from Tonga, China and Mongolia
- It's spiritually uplifting to hear that so many people want to help the needy and animals (and travel)
- It gave us the chance to see that beauty and brains were not mutually exclusive (well, almost)
- It gave us a chance to see loads of different girls in swimsuits without having to go to the beach or look at a Freeman's catalogue
- It's nice to see that among all the wars and fighting it is still possible for the world's most beautiful women to get together in love and harmony
- It was fun to invent your own judging system like 'Girl I'd most like to go through the *Kama Sutra* with' or 'Girl most likely to have been born a man'
- It gave judges the chance to have sex with up to 88 beautiful women (a chance you don't get every day)

MONEY — revealed! The only way to make money in today's society

- Dishonestly

MONKEY BUSINESS — frankly monkey-ist slurs that are spread about these creatures

- Orang-utans are notorious for their 'sharp' business practices
- Chimpanzees secretly own four out of the top five multi-national companies
- Gorillas are a franchise operation
- Baboons like nothing better than to trade in commodities when not swinging by their tails from a tree
- Gibbons invented state capitalism
- The real head of the CBI is a spider monkey called Chris
- Marmosets are not known for their financial acumen
- Woolly monkeys will short-change you, given half a chance
- Timeshare schemes were originally invented by the Guatemalan howler monkey
- In secret circles, the Bank of England is known as 'The Old Slow Loris of Threadneedle Street'

MOONING — what the oik performing this act may really be trying to communicate in his own primitive way

- 'Good evening, officer'
- 'My football team is better than your football team . . .'
- 'Don't talk to me about the European Community'
- 'I am enjoying myself at your wedding reception, Stephen'

- 'Are you enjoying your hen night, ladies?'
- 'And this one's going out to all the staff and customers here at McDonald's . . .'
- 'No, I do not wish to purchase a copy of *The Warcry*, madam . . .'
- 'I would like to resign from my present employment'
- 'I am not impressed by the nightlife Malaga has to offer'
- 'Your karaoke performance lacks a certain *je ne sais quoi*, I'm afraid . . .'
- 'So these are your private chambers, Judge. Now, quickly, take me, you sexy old QC, you!'

MOTHER THERESA — why Madonna is a better role model for today's women

- Madonna wears stylish Jean Paul Gaultier costumes, not an old dishcloth round her head
- Madonna wears a much bigger crucifix than Mother Theresa
- *Sex* sold over 2 million copies worldwide. Mother Theresa is still looking for a publisher for her version . . .
- Madonna helped raise millions of dollars when she sang on 'We are the World'; Mother Theresa didn't
- Madonna's video for 'Like a Prayer' was full of Catholic imagery; Mother Theresa has never done anything similar to spread the Gospel
- In 'Papa Don't Preach' Madonna pleads with her father not to criticise her for getting pregnant; Mother Theresa has never made a similar social comment
- Madonna has appeared on trendy TV programmes like *Wayne's World*; Mother Theresa hasn't even been asked
- Madonna is a Material Girl while Mother Theresa is a Spiritual Girl

- Madonna had a stormy relationship with Sean Penn; Mother Theresa has never dated anyone. Ever

MOTORWAYS — why we need more

- They'll take the pressure off the A roads
- And the existing motorways
- It'll be quicker for drivers to reach any remaining parks and woodlands
- So protest groups can get to Department of Transport public enquiries more easily
- So children get a chance to see more squashed animals and learn to identify them
- The government has got to use up all that road tax revenue somehow
- It will encourage people to travel and see more of this beautiful country
- If one motorway has major roadworks (anything involving 1,500 cones) there are alternative routes
- So that light aircraft have more of a choice of emergency landing sites if they run into difficulty
- While the Irish are building roads they're not building bombs

MPs — why it's good to serve your country as a Member of Parliament

- You get to nob unknown actresses
- You get to nob your secretary
- You get expensive gifts from greasy, slippery foreign businessmen
- The Commons bar is subsidised
- You know you'll never achieve anything, so you can take it nice and easy
- Powerful lobbies will pay through the nose for

you to put their point of view across in Parliament
- You can make 'wanker' signs across the floor at the Opposition, while pretending to wave your papers
- The more cracked you are, the more flamboyant you'll appear and the more successful you'll become
- You can leave your poxy constituency of Little-Shyte-in-the-Mire and move down to London where all the action is
- Parliamentary privilege allows you to say absolutely anything you like about absolutely anyone without fear of slander — you can quite happily say that your next-door neighbour enjoys conjugal rights with goats and exposes himself to nuns — and there's absolutely nothing he can do about it (apart from attack you with a claw hammer)

MUESLI — the most interesting thing about it

- It sounds like 'Spewsli'

MUGGING — how to avoid getting mugged

- Don't go out

NATIONAL ANTHEM — why it's rubbish

- There's no blistering guitar solo in the middle
- The drum roll at the beginning isn't exactly Cozy Powell
- The only reason the first three lines rhyme is because they all end with the same word
- No one can remember the second verse
- You have to sing it standing up, which is so tiring
- No one actually believes the lyrics
- It delays the start of football matches
- There's no version of it with rude words which you can sing instead
- Every time you sing it the Queen gets a royalty

THE NATIONAL HEALTH SERVICE — things it would be quite wrong of you to expect from it

- Annie Lennox on prescription
- An appointment within your lifetime
- An ambulance that reaches you in time
- Complete honesty when a routine operation goes drastically wrong

- Ambitious surgeons waiting until you're dead before stripping you of all your donor organs for their 'private patients'
- Compensation when some pissed anaesthetist destroys 95 per cent of your brain cells and you have to go through life typing with a metal rod strapped to your forehead
- Someone to come when you activate the nurse call system
- Agency nurses who could give a shit...
- The very latest treatment
- It still to exist in five years

NATIONS — 10 nations which don't matter

- Bhutan
- Iceland
- Andorra
- Portugal
- Tonga
- Burundi
- Chad
- Paraguay
- Australia
- Wales

NATURE LOVERS — things they conveniently forget

- Malaria-carrying insects
- Toads that look like Ivy in *Coronation Street*
- Stinging nettles
- Hay fever
- Wasps that get down the back of your shirt
- Tennyson's 'Nature red in tooth and claw'
- Toadstools
- Innocent golfers who are struck by lightning
- Deadly nightshade
- How boring it is in the countryside

NAZI WAR CRIMINALS — why they shouldn't have to stand trial

- They're trying to forget the war, so making them stand trial would only re-open painful wounds for them
- Most of the key witnesses to Nazi atrocities are dead and so wouldn't be able to testify
- Those that survived are so traumatised that their evidence wouldn't stand up in court
- You can't expect someone to remember what they were doing on a particular day 50 years ago
- If they did, two-thirds of Germany's senior managers would have to go to court, disrupting the country's economy

NEW MEN — things they should do to prove they're not wimps

- Scrawl suggestive graffiti all over Hennes swimwear posters
- Have girlfriends called Roxanne, Desiree or 'Chesty'
- Disseminate right-wing literature
- Refuse to stand to the right on escalators
- Get women pregnant for a laugh
- Read *Big Boobie Action*, *Hot Dyke Monthly* or *Shaven Hussies*
- Get pally with someone with a criminal record
- Light their own farts
- Stab someone in the back at work to get promotion
- Stab someone in the back
- Talk condescendingly to secretaries

NEPOTISM — why it's best to employ your relatives

- You can save stationery by including a written warning in their birthday cards
- You can take your family on holiday and legitimately claim it's an overseas business trip
- Threatening to write them out of your will is more effective than threatening them with the sack
- When you go to their house for dinner you'll be able to see if they've stolen any office supplies
- You can sleep with your secretary without feeling guilty because she's also your wife
- There's less chance of the staff forgetting your birthday
- It's easy to check if they're off sick — you just ring their parents
- Rather than calling an emergency board meeting to discuss a problem you can just wait until the next family wedding
- You know if their CV is accurate
- You can make sure your children do well by giving them huge pay rises

NOMADS — why they should be made to settle in one place

- Why let them leave a long trail of dirt and destruction when they can live in one permanent shithole?
- They're not where you expect them to be when you go looking for them
- They make world population statistics untidy
- If they were in one place, the law could keep tabs on what they really get up to with all those goats
- When you meet one and ask him where he's from, he can't give you a sensible answer

- 'Nomad' is a stupid occupation
- It looks even more stupid when written as your occupation on your passport
- Very few companies are presently looking to hire nomads, so they're making themselves unemployable
- They are presently depressing world property prices by not buying any houses
- Estate agents could make a come-back if all the nomads decided to settle down

THE NORTH — great northern inventions

- Mass unemployment
- Working men's clubs
- The phrase 'ey oop'
- Ram-raiding
- Black pudding
- Putting ferrets down your trousers
- The big 'brass band sound'
- The comedy and compassion of Thora Hird
- Back-to-backs

NORTH SEA — why we shouldn't worry about preserving the fish stocks

- Fish don't take the Pill, so they breed like Catholics
- If we caught less fish, they'd cost more in the shops
- We should take heart from the folk wisdom which tells us 'There's plenty more fish in the sea'
- If we don't catch the little finny bastards first, the French super-trawlers will get them
- Fish is 'brain food' — so it's obviously not very popular with the British public anyway
- Sometime soon, someone's going to catch on to the fact that the average North Sea fishfinger

now contains 20 per cent cod, 11 per cent toxic waste, 57 per cent used johnnies, 4 per cent human excrement, 2 per cent oil and 6 per cent driftwood, making them exceptionally unpopular

- In five years' time, there'll be nothing alive in the North Sea anyway
- When the North Sea's finished, there's always the Irish Sea and the Channel to fish out

NORWAY — support Norwegian whaling by buying their principal exports

- Haddock-scented shampoo and conditioner 2-in-1
- Eau de Fjord parfum de toilette
- Great woolly bobble hats with snowmen all round them
- Packets of crunchy Reindeer Scratchings
- Plastic trolls
- 'Big Halibut' — the aftershave for fishermen
- Snow
- Luxury minky whale soap-on-a-rope (It's 'blubbery' amazing!)
- A tree
- Some truly terrible Eurovision Song Contest single

NUCLEAR POWER — why it's ace

- It's better than burning orphans
- There's an almost sexual thrill about the dangers involved
- It helps to subsidise railway costs by using British Rail to secretly ship its waste products through your local station in the dead of night
- If Sellafield ever 'melts down', at least we'll take Communist China with us

- It's cheaper to keep than to dismantle and make safe

NUCLEAR WEAPONS — why Third World countries should build them

- What else are they going to do with all the plutonium that they've bought from the Middle East?
- Workers will become sterile handling radioactive material and this will bring the birthrate down
- While workers are building bombs they're not starving or begging
- It keeps the Atomic Energy Commission on their toes
- It will teach the West not to be complacent
- They can use them as bargaining tools for more Western aid
- It's cheaper to build bombs themselves than buy them ready-made

NUDITY — people we demand to see naked and we don't care how sexist it is

- Selina Scott
- Princess Di
- Beverly Craven
- Anthea Turner
- Mary Nightingale (!!!!!!!!!!!!!!)
- Belinda Carlisle
- Julia Roberts
- Annette Bening
- Ruby Wax (just to serve her right for humiliating everyone else)
- The Queen (just so we could tell everyone . . .)

NURSERY RHYMES — choice excerpts from the most politically incorrect

- 'Three blind mice, see how they run . . .'
- 'Four and twenty blackbirds, baked in a pie . . .'
- 'A-hunting we will go, a-hunting we will go . . .'
- 'Georgie Porgie, pudding and pie, kissed the girls and made them cry . . .'
- 'When the bow breaks, the cradle will fall . . .'
- 'The pig was eat and Tom was beat and Tom went howling down the street . . .'
- 'The grand old Duke of York, he had 10,000 men . . .'
- 'She gave them some broth without any bread. She whipped them all soundly and put them to bed'
- 'Baa baa black sheep . . .'

NURSES — why they don't mind being paid a pittance

- They get to wear sexy black stockings all day long
- They get the chance to see men's genitals (unless they're working in the Ear, Nose and Throat Ward or Maternity)
- There are plenty of opportunities to take advantage of tired, overworked junior doctors behind the screens
- If their boyfriends want them to dress up in a nurse's uniform they don't have to bother about buying one
- If a patient dies with no living relatives there's a good chance that the nurse will benefit from the will
- They get subsidised food at the hospital canteen
- They get a free colour TV (in most wards)
- Life in the nurses' quarters is one big giggle; like sharing a room with 120 of their mates
- They're used to it

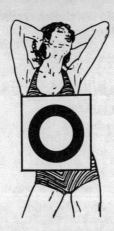

OBESE PEOPLE — why they should be made to lose weight — fast!

- They take up two seats on a bus, but only pay for one
- When you fancy a cream cake, there's never any left because some super-fatty's bought the entire stock
- It is not normal to have a bum 16 times the size of your head
- We can all live without opera. And sumo wrestling
- You get stuck in a queue at McDonald's because the Incredible Bulk in front of you has ordered 25 Big Breakfasts
- When they get ill, they have to be rushed to hospital by crane
- You invariably get stuck next to one on a long flight and spend the entire journey with your nose squashed painfully against the cabin window
- You can feel sympathy for someone whose downfall was pride or principles — but not Jaffa Cakes

- It would make more food available for the starving millions
- So we can all live in a brave new world that looks just like a Bacardi ad

OBSESSIVE CLEANLINESS SYNDROME — unkind things to say to sufferers

- 'After you've finished here, why don't you come round and start on my house?'
- 'God, it's filthy in here! You're a complete and utter pig!'
- 'I spy with my little eye a speck of dirt somewhere — can you see it?'
- 'It's all very well keeping your house spotless, but this street is filthy...'
- 'I hope you didn't mind me dropping round with my incontinent St Bernard like this...'
- 'I can smell something... I don't know what'
- 'The house looks great, Madge; but what's the attic like?'
- 'I've got a bottle of Domestos here in my bag. Right here. Right now. Fifty quid and it's yours...'
- 'Oh my God! Don't move. There's a cockroach in your kitchen!'
- 'Sorry, has it made a mess?'
- 'Have you seen the state of the Lebanon recently? Something should be done about it...'

OIL SLICKS — why it's good that sea birds get covered

- It discourages predators from eating them
- It provides them with a good disguise so they can creep up on fish at night
- It keeps them warm if they decide to swim the English Channel
- It stops their feathers becoming waterlogged

136

- You can take them home and fry them in their own oil
- If your car is about to seize up you can squeeze a few sea birds into the engine and carry on until you reach a garage
- It helps them float better when they're bobbing up and down in the sea
- Instead of having to transport oil by supertankers, major petro-chemical companies can now send over crates of birds for refining

OLD PEOPLE — why they're such miserable gits

- Chronic flatulence does very little for your temperament
- Incontinence trousers pinch your waist
- Give them a free bus pass and they think they're God
- Eating cat food sandwiches because your pension money is about to run out would put you in a foul mood too
- Their grandchildren only visit them for the money they give them
- Knowing they won't have a hip replacement operation until they're at least 104 makes them bitter and twisted
- They know the clock's ticking . . .
- You try getting a shag at 87
- You try shagging at 87
- So would you be if your wife looked like Captain Birdseye

ONE-PARENT FAMILIES — why they're good for you — a child's view

- There's only one adult to whack you if you misbehave
- There's plenty of room if you climb into your parent's double bed at night

- Grandparents over-compensate for your circumstances with loads of presents
- You can blame your circumstances for anything you do wrong
- Because your parent will more than likely stay in on Saturday nights you won't get stuck with some scabby babysitter
- Since there's only one adult to keep an eye on you you can get away with murder
- You only have to make a Father's Day or a Mother's Day card at school — not both

ONE-PARENT FAMILIES — what can we do to stop this blight on modern society

- Sterilise everyone called Tracy
- Vasectomise everyone called Darren
- Ban holidays in Malaga
- Bring back strictly single-sex schools
- Put itching powder in the backseats of the car whenever the kids want to borrow it for a date
- Play Rolf Harris's albums really loud outside your kid's room whenever they've got someone of the opposite sex in there
- Outlaw office parties
- Make sex illegal for those with an IQ under 100
- Teach children completely the wrong facts of life
- Raise the age of consent to 60

OPERA — 10 things more enjoyable to listen to

- Nails down a blackboard
- Knuckles being cracked
- Someone crashing into your new car
- The phone ringing at 6.30 a.m. on a Sunday morning
- A duet between Little Jimmy Osmond and Sonia
- Any rave record

- Your neighbour's cat under the rear wheels of your car
- Your front door being kicked down at 5 a.m. by four men from Customs & Excise

ORGANIC FARMING — why it's shit

- Because it is

OXFAM — 15 of the crappiest ethnic products you should avoid buying from there

- Ugly squiggly grubby little rugs that are supposed to encapsulate culture in the Andes (perhaps they do)
- A black carved animal that might be a pig, a hippo, or a dinosaur
- A dangly bit of multi-coloured rope which can have no possible use whatsoever
- Some sort of gaily coloured pipe you'd never dare use in your local — or in front of a policeman
- Candles (very precious, no doubt, in Equador, but not so interesting in a country with modern electric lighting)
- Carved African wooden faces that all look like Frances de la Tour
- Something blobby and indescribable made out of paper and black lacquer
- Some ethnically decorated bag it took a peasant five minutes to knock up and five seconds for you to realise how vile it is
- Wooden serving spoons that look like they've been rescued from a house fire
- Drinks coasters woven from hemp that are so uneven you daren't even rest a tumbler on them
- Leather belts suitable only for someone with an 18-inch waist
- A copper bracelet so naff that even the one that

your granny wears to prevent rheumatism has more style
- A hand-carved wooden doll so hideous that it would make children wet the bed
- A clay pot that looks like it was removed from the kiln halfway through the firing
- Tatty old raffia baskets

PACKAGING — why having lots of it is good

- It makes the product look that much more expensive (important if it's a gift)
- It makes you believe that the manufacturers actually care about what they sell
- Children like to use old boxes to make armoured personnel carriers, stealth bombers and other educational toys
- It helps manufacturers disguise the fact that the product on the inside looks nothing like the picture on the outside
- And is five times smaller than portrayed
- Because most of it ends up in the landfill tips it provides a use for the countryside
- It makes you believe that the product will actually last a long time
- If Easter eggs were just sold loose in a brown paper bag, no one would buy them
- Ever tried to get a new TV set that was just wrapped in newspaper home?
- Ever played Pass the Parcel with just one layer of tissue paper?

MODERN PAGANS — things they believe in

- Dancing naked at a full moon will help you with a job application
- Worshipping at Stonehenge on the Summer Solstice will make you lucky in the latest Reader's Digest prize draw
- If you put your head next to a toad and listen to it, it will tell you what's on TV tonight
- Smearing your body with equal amounts of woad and cowshit will repair your IBM-compatible PC when it crashes
- Reciting the ancient chants of the Druids will help your car to start in cold weather
- It is perfectly respectable to buy an altar table from Ikea
- The gods and goddesses will not be offended if you practise safe sex at orgies
- Drinking the blood of a sacrificial goat is cruel and specist, and that a cup of carrot juice is just as acceptable
- Ancient stones and trees are really alive and know a lot of the people you know

PANDAS — why they're such crap at sex

- Female pandas don't fancy male pandas — they fancy Mel Gibson
- Male pandas don't fancy female pandas — they fancy Mel Gibson, too
- When they were cubs, their parents didn't explain the facts of life to them
- They live in China and, being good Communists, know that having more than one offspring is a serious offence
- Not one panda owns a copy of Marvin Gaye's 'Sexual Healing' — so seduction is impossible in the panda world

- They'd much rather nibble bamboo than a mate's earlobe
- Pandas live on steep mountain slopes and after an exhausting day traversing them, the last thing they feel up to is a bit of slap and tickle
- There are no panda discos, dating agencies or singles clubs
- Pandas don't drink, and so very rarely have the courage to proposition other pandas
- If you were in a cage, with hundreds of people all chanting 'Go on, give her one!', you'd feel the pressure too

PARENTS — controversial but undeniable uses for them in later life

- Sources of milk, butter, cheese, eggs or whatever else you happen to run out of and can't be arsed to shop for
- Sources of giant, interest-free loans you have no intention of paying back
- Inheritances
- Babysitting your kids while you're out enjoying yourself
- Someone you can fall back on when your Visa card bill gets out of hand
- A free source of Christmas dinner (and Boxing Day, if you play your cards right)
- Someone you can always run home to when your partner decides they can't stand life with you any more
- Someone to knit your little 'uns' entire wardrobe, free
- People who know how to fix the plumbing, mend the car, repair the electrics, creosote a fence, wallpaper the hall — and just about every other practical task you could never be bothered to master

PARENTS BY POST — why it's a waste of time to sponsor a kid in Colombia

- They never remember to phone you on your birthday
- They won't look after you when you're old
- How do you know they're going to spend your £20 a month on books and clothes and not sweets or computer games?
- They'll probably turn up on your doorstep unannounced with 20 of the village elders, all wanting to stay
- They'll start resenting you because you never see them
- You might get a visit one day from the Colombian social services asking why you haven't made sure your child's been going to school
- You can't claim for Child Benefit

PARENTS BY POST — why it doesn't have to be a waste of time sponsoring a kid in Colombia

- He'll probably end up a key player in the Medellín cartel in a few years' time and will be able to show his gratitude with 100-kilo bags of uncut cocaine

PENIS — why it's good to have one

- It's a man's world
- You'd look sad in swimming trunks without one
- It gives you something to do in your spare time
- You can take it out in pubs after six pints
- You can use it to urinate down walls after eight pints
- You won't suffer from penis envy — probably
- It means you're not a woman
- Or a solicitor

PENSIONS — why the elderly should no longer receive them

- It's such a pittance anyway that no one will notice they've stopped
- Old people won't be able to run their cars any more which means we won't have to get stuck behind an M-registered Austin Allegro or Triumph Dolomite going at 28 mph
- They also won't be able to afford to keep their scabby old dogs, making the streets a cleaner place to walk in
- We're sick of paying for them out of our National Insurance contributions
- They're not in the least bit grateful for it
- If they want money they should work for it like the rest of us; there are plenty of suitable jobs for pensioners, like lollipop ladies and scarecrows
- It's a well-known fact that OAPs just squander *our* money away at bingo
- They waste great wads of it on crap like cat food, haemorrhoid cream and presents for the grandchildren
- One in ten pensioners doesn't make it home with their pension without getting mugged, so that's money down the drain
- If people know that old people don't have any money then they won't rob them while posing as Water Board officials
- If they want money, they should have worked harder when they were younger
- They're going to die soon anyway; if you were a bank, would you keep pumping money into a company that was certain to fail?
- Being absent-minded, they often forget they've got the money
- By the time we get to a pensionable age, you can be sure some Tory government or other will

have done away with the state pension altogether, so why should their generation get preferential treatment?

PEOPLE — good people to pick on, just for the fun of it

- The fat
- The thin
- The ugly
- Wig-wearers
- Trainspotters
- Four-eyed gits
- People with funny teeth
- Brainboxes who have swallowed a dictionary or something
- People what speak funny (except Arnold Schwarzenegger)
- Anyone smaller and less bolshie than yourself

PEOPLE — bad people to pick on, just for the fun of it

- Anyone with a gun
- Yourself
- Your big brother
- Anyone two feet taller than you
- Professional boxers
- Members of the SAS
- Someone you desperately want to go out with
- Anyone with a tattoo on their forehead
- An entire Hells Angels chapter
- Daffy Duck (he doesn't exist)

PHARMACEUTICAL COMPANIES — why they should be congratulated

- They draw our attention to the dangers of releasing new drugs that haven't been adequately tested — eventually

- They don't test all their new drugs on animals
- They give loads of money in compensation to victims of their drugs
- They keep teams of lawyers permanently in work
- They take poor, overworked doctors on all-expenses-paid trips to the Caribbean
- They invented side effects
- They've boldly continued the experiments started by World War II Nazi scientists

PIGS — why they deserve to be eaten

- They spend their days rolling in shit. (All right, they are naturally clean animals and it's farmers who put them in those conditions, but it's still pretty disgusting)
- They'd eat you if they could, if only they were twice the size, had canine teeth and weren't herbivores
- They're ugly and not very cuddly
- They taste great
- They're fat little bastards, perfect for a high meat yield
- Their name is perfectly suited to their lifestyle
- George Orwell thought pigs were fascists — and he knew his onions, politically speaking
- They're the only animal you can make bacon from
- They're selfish little gits. They know they're going to die a few hours before they're butchered, so they release a strong stress chemical which spoils their juicy porky taste. The effect is called PSE (pale, soft and exudative)

PLACES — 10 places in Britain that the Politically Correct would just love to rename . . .

- Personchester (Manchester)
- Person-of-racepool (Blackpool)

- Temporally challenged Pig Flesh (Oldham)
- Phallo-repressivefosters (Cockfosters)
- Spinster-by-choicestone (Maidstone)
- Female Parentwell (Motherwell)
- The Isle of Person (The Isle of Man)
- Existentially deprivemarnock (Kilmarnock)
- Academically challenged-enhead (Birkenhead)
- Isle of Person of Noncolour (The Isle of Wight)

POLICE CODES — America's most politically incorrect codes, which could easily be adopted over here

- 154 = Lone black motorist with no video camera in the vicinity
- 225 = Young black male acting suspiciously innocuously
- 434 = Puerto Rican in possession of a hat. Request permission to use lethal force if necessary
- 226 = Black family in need of assistance. Please disregard call
- 479 = Police bribe in progress. No drive-bys in this area for next 45 minutes
- 398 = Middle-aged black man acting suspiciously with hamburger
- 543 = Harmless blind black beggar in need of vigorous beating
- 821 = Attention all units. Alibi needed for drunk cop who's just shot a five-year-old black kid for a dare
- 735 = Young Hispanic male in need of drugs planting on him to improve arrest rate
- 593 = Officer down. Will be finished with prostitute in five minutes

THE POLAR ICECAPS — why their melting will be a blessing in disguise

- Ninety-eight per cent of Belgium will be under 400 feet of water
- There'll never be a repeat of the *Titanic* tragedy
- All the penguins will fall into the sea, the whales will gobble them up and there won't be a shortage of whales any more
- Michael Palin won't be able to go there at the licence payer's expense
- Nineteen billion cubic tonnes of new fresh water might reduce the pollution in the North Sea by a couple of per cent
- Face it, they're not much use as they are
- Polar bears will be bloody grateful they're in a zoo for a change, instead of treading water

POLICE FORCE — why it should be halved

- It would reduce the number of cases of wrongful arrest
- It would halve the number of complaints against the police
- Fewer suspects would fall downstairs in police cells
- Gangs of vigilantes would be able to work more freely
- Fewer arrests would show that crime was decreasing
- There'd be more money in backhanders for the officers remaining
- It would halve the number of road accidents

THE POLITICALLY CORRECT — how to taunt them

- We outnumber you 10,000 to 1!
- You don't see many McDonald's closing down, do you?

- Hey bitch, wanna come upstairs and see my fur jockstrap?
- Hunters One, Fox Nil!
- I killed a tree the other day
- The Tories just keep on winning!
- Do you think my leather sofa matches my mahogany panelling?
- I bagged that one while on safari in Kenya last year!
- My loft isn't insulated. Want a fight about it?
- Sting's going bald!

POLLUTION IN RIVERS — why it's beneficial

- Fish are easier to catch when they're floating on the surface
- Hey, the rivers look like a psychedelic rippling torrent of rainbow colours, man. Far out
- If the companies weren't allowed to discharge into rivers, they would probably empty their effluent in your front garden secretly at night
- If you accidentally fall in, you won't drown — you'll just be transformed into an 8-foot shambling hulk of toxic waste sludge
- When you go on a boating holiday, you needn't worry about the smell of your chemical toilets — the smell of the river will block them out
- It's so corrosive, it breaks down all the old tyres and shopping trolleys people dump into the river
- In two years time, all those pompous Hooray Henrys at the Henley Regatta are going to have to wear gas masks ... Try drinking champagne and eating caviar through one of those muthas, dickheads!
- Swans are vicious bastards — who needs them?
- It's killed all the otters — putting an end to the cruel sport of otter-hunting

- It gets washed out to sea and we can share it with all our European neighbours

POOPER-SCOOPERS — why we shouldn't use them

- It'll stink out your dustbin when you get home
- The rain will wash the dog's muck away anyway
- Any kid stupid enough to play with dogshit deserves all they get, matey
- Wild animals shit everywhere, but no one complains about that
- When you consider that most parks now are littered with discarded needles and crack phials, it's pretty pointless clearing up some dog's muck
- Pooper-scoopers are another way of getting us to do what the council refuse department really should be doing
- Do drunks carry 'Vom-per-scoopers' to clear up the puddles they leave outside your house?

THE POOR — why they will always be with us

- Everybody gets old
- Jesus himself said so — and who's to argue with Him?
- Someone will always have to do the unpopular, badly paid jobs
- If there weren't poor people, rich people wouldn't be rich
- Someone has to buy clothes at Woolworth's
- It's against the law to shoot them
- Publishers' royalties
- If you gave everything you had to the poor — you'd be poor yourself, so it wouldn't help a bit, would it?

PORNOGRAPHY — why it's good

- It gives you the horn

POSITIVE DISCRIMINATION — 10 things that blind people shouldn't be allowed to participate in

- Formula One motor racing
- Pistol shooting
- Cross-country skiing
- Dancing on a crowded dance floor
- Playing 'chicken' in traffic
- Heavyweight boxing
- Interior decorating
- Open-heart surgery
- The public demonstration of a brand-new type of chainsaw
- Spot welding

POST TRAUMATIC STRESS SYNDROME — some politically incorrect terms for sufferers

- Cowardy custard
- Yellow belly
- Jelly on a plate
- Big girl's blouse
- Scaredy cat
- Chicken
- Mr Shit His Pants
- Cry baby
- Mummy's boy
- Sissy

POTTING BIRDS — why it's ripping good fun

- They go 'AWWWWKKKKKKKKKKK!' when you hit one
- They go 'EEEEKKKKKKKKKKK!' when you wing one
- Sometimes they completely explode and disintegrate in mid-air, drawing gasps of admiration from your fellow shooters
- There's a strong element of personal danger involved, as there should be in all the best

sports — you might actually get crapped on if you don't have your wits about you
- Sometimes they're not dead and you get to finish them off with your boots
- You can pretend you're really shooting at flying oiks
- You get to meet all sorts of important people when shooting, like Princes Philip and Charles (Head of the Worldwide Fund for Nature and a renowned nature lover respectively)

POWER — politically incorrect suggestions for alternative methods of power generation

- A giant handle cranked incessantly by the entire population of Wales
- Furnaces powered by the cremation of stray dogs
- Electrodes attached to the right hands of pre-pubescent boys (and most men). Think of it as a form of 'wave' power
- Burning the prized possessions of elderly people who are forced into homes
- A method which taps the hot air expelled constantly by taxi drivers (from both orifices)
- Unemployed people shovelling out-of-circulation £50 notes into boilers
- Unemployed people shovelling repossessed items into boilers
- Steam turbines kept boiling by the rage and dissatisfaction of ordinary people
- Harnessing the coughing of long-term smokers

PREGNANT WOMEN — why we shouldn't give up our seats on the train for them

- They knew what they were letting themselves in for when they got pregnant
- Standing is better for the circulation and helps the baby develop

- Really fat people don't expect passengers to give up their seats for them
- They're probably sitting or lying down for most of the day so standing makes them exercise the muscles they wouldn't normally use
- One of the old wives' tales about pregnancy is 'If the mother stands tall and straight, baby will be of normal weight. But if she sits near to the ground, baby will be forty pounds'. And you can't argue with that
- They might not be pregnant at all and might just have a cushion stuck up their dress in a ruse to get a seat
- It takes less effort for them to get off the train from a standing position
- Where would we stop? Women with ovarian cysts? Women with periods? Women whose lipstick is smudged a bit?
- You only need to give up your seat to someone who's pregnant *and* an old-age pensioner

THE PRESIDENT OF THE UNITED STATES — politically incorrect things to say to him

- 'You're doing a damn fine job; carry on just the way you are'
- 'Go on, press it! I dare you!'
- 'Do you realise how much you could save by cutting food stamps?'
- 'I bumped into Saddam Hussein today and he called you an Infidel Capitalist-Poof Dog. Now, where I come from, that's fighting talk, son . . .'
- 'Foreign aid, schmoreign aid . . .'
- 'Sir, if we don't use the Marines on someone soon, they're going to go stir crazy . . .'
- 'Before you help the needy, let me say just three little letters — J-F-K'
- 'If that doesn't convince you, what about three others — M-L-K?'

- 'Go on, just one more aircraft carrier; we could call it the USS *Clinton* . . .'
- 'Listen, I'm head of the CIA — and if I say you dance the hornpipe naked on the White House lawns, Billy-Boy, you goddamn do it!'

PRIME MINISTERS — why we should never allow another woman to become Prime Minister

- Margaret Thatcher

PRIME MINISTERS — why we should never allow another man to become Prime Minister

- John Major

PRIME MINISTERS — why we should never allow another person of either gender to become Prime Minister

- Edward Heath

PRISONERS OF CONSCIENCE — why they're wimps

- Not one of them has a nickname like 'Killer', 'Dutch' or 'Scarface'
- The worst thing they've ever done is write a poem criticising the army, not shooting dead three policemen
- They'd rather wait for international pressure to get them released, not three of their mates, a bazooka and a helicopter
- They think the pen is mightier than the sword
- They keep protesting about their sentence rather than accepting their punishment for the risk they took
- Their regular visitor is some weedy bloke from Amnesty International, not a peroxide blonde

moll with a short skirt and a surprise tucked away in her knickers
- While everyone else is smuggling tobacco in, they're smuggling letters out

'PROBLEM CHILDREN' — what can we do about them?

- Make it against the law for thick adults to reproduce
- Put them in a special school with other problem children — and a large assortment of sharp kitchen implements
- Invite them to the hospital to try out the new SuperNES — and then sneak up behind them and lobotomise them
- Sell them to American couples who are desperate to adopt
- Give them a plastic bag and some glue and let nature take its course
- Rig our cars to explode when one of the little scrotes attempts to steal it
- Revert to the government policy of 'a short sharp shock' – this time using 20,000 volts
- Try understanding them — and when that fails shoot the little sods
- Show them their victims and the results of their actions. Then when they're busy pissing themselves laughing, bring a large piece of heavy furniture down on their heads

'PROBLEM CHILDREN' — things they don't respond to

- Love
- Tolerance
- Understanding
- Logic
- Appeals to their better nature

- Kindness
- Compassion
- Education
- The benefit of the doubt
- One last chance

'PROBLEM CHILDREN' — things that they do respond to

- Severe violence
- An XR3i with the keys still in the ignition
- Glue
- Easy money
- Your handbag
- Video nasties
- Alcohol
- A gun to the head

PROSTITUTION — why it should be legalised

- So High Court judges and DPPs wouldn't get into so much trouble
- Men wouldn't feel so uncomfortable about the whole thing
- It gives any woman the chance to have sex with as many different men as she likes (whey-hey!)
- If you're not satisfied with a prostitute, instead of beating her up you can take your grievance to the Trading Standards Officer
- So you can get a receipt for tax purposes (like if you're researching this book, for example)
- It will help to maintain standards and rates throughout the country. For example, a 'quick one' in Manchester is noticeably longer than a 'quick one' in Bradford: There is also confusion when it comes to the subject of 'manual relief'. In Hull, a 'hand shandy' uses all fingers, while only the thumb and forefinger are employed in Bournemouth and many other South Coast towns

157

- MPs will be able to go on 'fact-finding missions' to Amsterdam and the Reeperbahn on taxpayers' money

PROVERBS — some of the most politically incorrect

- Money talks, people mumble
- A woman's place is in the home
- A woman, a dog and a walnut tree — the more you beat them the better they be
- A rich man can do nothing wrong
- He that has a wife, has strife
- After shaking hands with a Greek, count your fingers
- There's no fool like an old fool
- A man without money is no man at all
- Money is the only monarch
- Ugly women, finely dressed, are the uglier for it
- God help the rich, the poor can beg
- You may beat a horse till he be sad, and a cow till she be mad
- It is better to want meat than guests or company
- Boys will be boys
- Wine makes old wives wenches
- They that are bound must obey
- The pot calling the kettle black

THE PUB — how to behave with precise political incorrectness on the way home from your local

- Try sticking two fingers down your throat and puking up in a shop doorway. (Always the sign of a good lads' night out)
- Hawk violently and then spit on the pavement every 20 yards or so
- Run in front of any car you see with women in it, stick your tongue out and waggle it

- Take a leak standing up against a parked car, shop front or garden wall
- If passing a residential area where you know people are asleep, make the loudest unintelligible animal noises you can
- Use the C word whenever possible
- Scream 'Wanker!' every seven paces, for reasons best known to yourself
- If you come across an expensive car, either exclaim, 'Worrrr! Fucking tasty motor, that!' or get your keys out and scratch it
- Stumble over milk bottles, even if you have to go into someone's porch to do so
- If you come across an unaccompanied woman, be sure to leer right up into her face, exclaim, 'Worrrr! You're a tasty bird, you!' and then ask her to show you her white bits or, alternatively, if she 'Wants to do it'
- Lastly, always make sure you've got piss stains on your shoes

PUBLIC SCHOOLS — why it's better to go to one than a state school

- If you go to a state school it's unlikely you'll end up sharing a locker with an heir to a throne
- At a public school your rugby coach is more likely to be an ex-England prop-forward than an ex-RAF PE teacher or someone just released from Pentonville
- If you're invited back to friends' for tea you can play tennis, go bowling, swimming and jet-skiing without leaving the house or its grounds
- If one of your classmates says his dad has three Aston Martins and a private jet it's probably true and you won't need to call him a 'lying toe rag'. Whereas in a state school if someone says they've got a dad, you *know* they're lying

- Your school trip is more likely to be to the Masai Mara game reserve than London Zoo
- You're more likely to end up serving on the bench — not sleeping on one
- The drug scene is more likely to revolve around coke and heroin than a canister of lighter fuel and a tube of UHU

PUBLIC TRANSPORT — why it's a bad idea

- Other members of the public can use it
- Some git with the world's loudest Walkman sits next to you and proceeds to play with his Gameboy
- You discover that someone's spat or puked up on your seat — when you arrive home and your partner asks what's that on the back of your jeans
- It's more dangerous to use public transport these days than it is to walk home
- The person standing next to you hasn't washed since the days of the threepenny bit
- Somewhere behind you a child is being repeatedly hit by its mother for crying
- You get tired of the grime, the filth, the smell and the relentless swaying — and that's only your fellow passengers
- Pensioners get to use it free — and hog all the seats. Mind you, with all the puke and spit and chewing gum on them, they're quite welcome
- Your bus or carriage is always the one the loony decides to get on and immediately recognises you as a lifelong friend . . .

PUPPIES — why it's good to give them for Christmas

- They don't require batteries
- You don't need to assemble them the night before

- They're cheaper than a Sega Mega Drive
- And marginally quieter
- They (probably) won't break by Boxing Day
- You won't get pissed off seeing them greatly reduced in the January sales
- They won't be out of date two months later
- You won't be worried about your kid getting epilepsy through playing with them all day
- It'll get your kids out of doors and in the fresh air
- If no one likes it, you can always dump it on a motorway

THE QUEEN — things she simply will not comprehend in a million years

- Poverty
- Hunger
- Suffering
- Having the phone cut off
- Struggling to pay the mortgage on Buck House
- Republicanism
- French kissing
- Beans on toast
- Going to work by bus
- Promotion
- Ambition
- Putting the empties out at night
- What Andrew ever saw in that oiky blousy Fergie woman
- Why all the riff-raff sleeping rough in London don't smarten themselves up and sort themselves out

QUORN — why it's such a good food

- Being a 'small relative of the mushroom' it probably has hallucinogenic properties which make you believe you're eating something appetising
- It comes from a long line of tasty foods that begin with 'Q' like quails and . . . um . . . er . . .
- It's got the same name as the hunt Prince Charles rides with in Leicestershire so it must be good
- It's got twice the appeal of a 'meat' dish made out of soya
- You could easily mistake it for steak (if you were completely sensorally challenged)
- It makes a good triple word score in Scrabble
- It helps keep your weight down (mainly because you can't bear to eat anything made with it)
- It costs so much that it must be good

RABBITS — one good reason why rabbits should have shampoo squirted in their eyes

- It teaches them how humans would feel if the shampoo wasn't tested on rabbits first

THE RAIN FORESTS — why they're crap

- Who wants to go where it's always raining?
- When you've seen one tree you've seen them all
- They're full of spiders bigger than your head
- Any place where you stand a good chance of getting a blow dart in the neck must be worth avoiding
- Nowhere accepts sterling travellers' cheques
- The nearest Pizza Hut is 12,000 miles away and anyway, you'd be outside their free delivery area
- If they were any good then they'd be called the 'sunshine forests'
- You'll bump into Sting and he'll insist on playing you the demos for his new album

RAM RAIDING — why it's OK

- It enables you to show your dissatisfaction with the shop's pricing policy
- It enables you to test out the crumple zones on the car you've just stolen
- It enables you to shop after hours
- It's easier than walking out with three colour TVs under your coat
- There's no chance of getting your collar felt by store detectives
- You can see whether something's in stock right away
- It's not as if you're holding up the shop with a sawn-off shotgun
- No staff are at risk (unless they're window dressing at the time)
- It gives the owner of the car that's been stolen the chance to see it one last time on *Crimestoppers*

'READERS' WIVES' – why they're a good idea

- It keeps Polaroid in profit
- It's surprising how many people like to see out-of-focus photos in a magazine
- It shows everyone what awful taste you have in carpets
- It lets readers say to themselves, 'Cor, wouldn't touch yours, mate!'
- It enables pornographic magazines to fill four pages very cheaply
- It lets you see the very latest ranges from MFI
- It lets you see what all that lingerie sold in petrol stations really looks like on someone
- They increase the sale of bananas
- And Sellotape (to stop the breasts sagging)
- They let unmarried men see what women with stretch marks look like

RECOVERY — irrefutable proof that the Tories have finally got the economic recovery under way

- A couple came to view a flat in Solihull last week
- Someone bought a pack of video cassettes in Winchester Woolworth's Tuesday lunchtime — and *almost* bought a box of Cadbury's Misshapes at the same time!
- Five men and two women from the South East found jobs last month
- Someone looked at a new camera in Dixons in Coventry on Thursday
- Six extra packets of salt 'n' vinegar crisps were exported this month — an upturn of 50 per cent
- Only one major shipyard closed down this month
- The unemployment total in Cardiff plunged by two, compared to last month!
- Tie Rack sold an extra tie in its UK outlets this week
- The Imperial Cancer Research Fund reported more 5p pieces than 2p pieces in their collecting tins for the first time in five years
- There has been a decline of 14 per cent in the demand for large cardboard boxes, sleeping bags, blankets and woolly balaclavas

RECYCLING — why it's a waste of time

- Think of all the petrol you waste driving to the local refuse dump
- Who wants to spend thousands on a new car that's probably got bits of a D-reg Lada in it?
- You waste untold energy sorting all your bottles into different coloured glass
- When you try to separate the rubbish into different categories every week you're likely to

get congealed cat food all over your hands — or sever your thumb on the tin can it came in

- When glass bottles are refilled how can you be sure that the strawberry jam you just bought hasn't got any rancid pickled onions still stuck to the bottom of the jar?
- Dustmen demand higher wages because they've now become Refuse Management Executives
- Recycled paper always smells of its previous role in life — just as any greetings card you buy always smells like a take-away kebab

REFUGEES — how the Home Office can tell a genuine political refugee from an economic migrant

- Genuine refugees have no fingernails
- They flinch whenever you flick on a light switch
- They hide behind chairs when you produce some everyday object, like a corkscrew
- They don't bring their families and dependants with them — because they're all dead or 'missing'
- Their testicles probably don't add up to two
- Or one
- They wake up screaming and sweating at night
- They dive for cover when a car backfires
- They've already been rejected for sanctuary by Germany

REFUSE MANAGEMENT EXECUTIVES — some politically incorrect (but more accurate) names for these invaluable members of society

- Dustmen
- Bin men
- Those bastards who forgot to empty your bin this week

- Those bastards who didn't turn up this week — again
- 'Jobsworth' arseholes who won't take away anything that isn't strictly speaking 'in the bin' (unless it's your child's bike and their kid has a birthday coming up)
- The bastards who wake you up with all that clatter at 7 a.m.
- The people who block the entire road so you're stuck behind them for 20 minutes
- Clumsy oafs who spill more rubbish in the gutter than they succeed in tipping in the back of their dustcart
- Those filthy gits who spilled rubbish all over your front lawn
- Those berks with the nerve to ask for a Christmas box for fouling your lawn and driveway all year

RELIGIOUS CULTS — why it's good to join one

- If you're a weak-willed loser, it gives you a purpose in life
- You get the chance to have more than one sexual partner (and variety is the spice of life)
- You never need to wear your Sunday best
- You get the chance to meet hundreds of like-minded people
- You don't have to worry about keeping up with the Joneses because everyone has to renounce their possessions
- You also don't have to worry about keeping up with the Joneses because they all killed themselves with poisoned Kool Aid in Guyana a few years ago
- If someone doesn't like your point of view you can shoot them rather than enter into a lengthy ideological debate

- By never seeing your family you can save loads of money on birthday presents
- You can die in a blaze of glory (knowing you've wrecked the career of the head of the FBI)
- Your leader will be able to provide you with a religious context for all those sexual acts you previously found repulsive, unnatural and unhygienic — and personally help you to overcome your prejudices against them

RELIGIOUS CULTS — good rituals to practise

- RAMAKRISHNA — Remarkably like 'postman's knock', except that it isn't called that
- RAMARAMA — A nirvana-seeking version of 'spin the bottle'
- KRISHNARAMA — This involves dancing rhythmically to 1960s soul music while drinking exotic cocktails with umbrellas, sparklers and slices of fruit in them
- KRISHNARAMAKALI — For this ritual, you must lie down stark naked and be covered in fresh fruit segments. Your female disciples should then eat the fruit from the various parts of your anatomy while you approach nirvana and try to understand the true meaning of this ritual . . .
- KALIRAMA — Your disciples must learn the meaning of humility. Have them do your washing and shopping while you make a point of conspicuously sitting around eating lots of Ferrero Rocher chocolates and watching MTV
- KALIKALI — The wearing of stockings and suspenders by all female members of the sect in recognition of our own mortality (or something)
- KALIRAMAKRISHNA — The initiation speech given to all new male members, the holy words of which go something like; 'My son, your soul can only be unburdened of its karmic weight

by the generous donation of all your wordly
goods to me — don't cross the cheque — and
first dibs on your girlfriend'

RELIGIOUS FUNDAMENTALISM — why it's so good

- You save time by not having to contemplate
  anyone else's point of view
- Being right about everything is very good for
  building your self-confidence
- It gives you plenty of opportunities to beat
  yourself in public without feeling embarrassed
- Covering up women's faces means you can play
  a game trying to guess who they are
- And sleeping with other women — by mistake,
  of course
- It gives you the excuse you need to hold
  Westerners hostage
- By burning the emblems of Western
  governments you can learn all the different
  flags of the world
- You get plenty of photo opportunities on the
  international news — especially if you jump up
  and down, foaming at the mouth and scream
  'Down with Clinton, the great Satan!'
- It's reassuring to know that you support the best
  god in the entire universe

RHINO HORNS — some good uses for them

- A coat hook
- Needle for your record deck
- Somewhere to hang your umbrella
- Hollow it out and use it as an ear trumpet
- Or an ice-cream cone
- Put elastic round the base and wear it as a silly
  hat
- Put elastic round the base and wear it as an
  imitation Ralph Halpern nose

- Stuff it down your pants and impress the girls
- A dildo

RHYMING SLANG — some politically incorrect examples

- Sweet wrapper = Slapper
- Plum and sago = Dago
- Finger click = Spick
- Pint of stout = Kraut
- Wooden clog = Frog
- Ear infection = Vivisection
- Gareth Hunt = Vagina
- Talking shit = Cockney git

RICH — why it's good to be really wealthy

- People write you begging letters and you can write back to them saying, 'Go away, poor person'
- You can put a sticker in the back of your Rolls-Royce saying 'My Other Car's A Rolls-Royce Too'
- You can drive your Ferrari Testarossa up and down outside the Skoda showroom, making the less well off feel really inadequate
- You can be as crazy as a loon and everyone will humour you instead of shutting you in a bin somewhere
- Your bank manager will take you seriously
- Your local MP will take you seriously
- You can get adequate medical treatment when you need it

ROBIN HOOD — why he was politically incorrect

- He was a thief
- He wanted to kill the king
- He was a member of the privileged aristocracy
- He killed animals and used their hides for clothing

- His Merry Men were exclusively white Anglo-Saxon males and didn't include any disabled persons (not at first, anyway)
- He tried to impress women with daring exploits rather than being sensitive to their needs
- He gave cruel nicknames to his friends Little John and Friar Tuck just because they were vertically advantaged and circumferentially challenged
- He also named one of his men Will Scarlet because of his acute eczema
- The forest he lived in was not properly managed
- The most famous actor to play him, Errol Flynn, was later exposed as a Nazi spy

THE ROAD TO HELL — what it's probably really paved with, instead of 'good intentions'

- Discarded kebab papers
- Dog shit
- Ice-lolly wrappers
- Those mysterious yellow-orange splatters of vomit that appear overnight, like crop circles
- Broken glass
- McDonald's cartons
- Crumpled cans of lager
- More dog shit
- A big juicy unmissable gob
- Upturned supermarket trollies

THE ROYAL FAMILY — why it's good we have one

- If there was no Royal Family, nothing would ever get opened, Colours would never be trooped and stamps would be blank and therefore easy to forge
- They're so gracious and good-mannered, except for that awful Fergie woman and they've got rid of her now

- In the very same year that the Queen had her Annus Horribilis we all had our Annus Fucking Horribilis too, which means she's really one of us
- Were they to be deposed, Buckingham Palace would be full of squatters in a week
- They prove that the country's medical facilities are really top rate when they want to be — the Queen Mum only has to have hiccups for a helicopter to be there to rush her to hospital. Isn't it reassuring to know that that kind of speed of response and professionalism is available to you and your elderly relatives too?
- Tourists come to this stinking rat hole of a country specifically to see them
- They serve as a proof of the dangers of inbreeding
- They help struggling comedy writers by providing a rich source of amusement

ROYALTY — Prince Charles's top politically incorrect turn-ons

- A shrub in a low-cut dress
- Hyacinths with a flirty nature
- Begonias with long, long tendrilly roots
- A tree that looks like it's been around
- Demure sweet peas
- A weeping willow that wants to be kissed better
- A pot plant that takes the initiative in the bedroom
- Two young carnations cross-pollinating in a secluded bower
- Easy conifers
- Tulips with whopping big stamens
- A hydrangea caught photosynthesising

THE 'RURAL IDYLL' — what it really consists of

- Tedium
- The smell of manure, morning, noon and night
- Whole villages of people who are all related to one another in lots of strange ways
- The Hunt trampling straight across your beautiful landscape garden, churning up the lawn and chewing up your cats
- People who look at you funny
- People who just look funny
- Demented farmers looking for an excuse to shoot your dog with both barrels
- A bus into town that appears as often as Halley's Comet
- Some witless farm labourer banging on your door saying, 'Combine harvester's taken me arm off, ma'am. Can I store it in 'e fridge?'
- A painful and premature death from the experimental pesticide the local farmer's been trying out

SALMAN RUSHDIE — why we should turn him over to the Iranians

- They've asked for him and it would be impolite to refuse

RUSSIA — why it's such a crap place to live

- Everywhere is downwind of Chernobyl
- Before Chernobyl their greatest technological achievement was some stupid wooden dolls that fitted inside each other
- The best car you can buy is a Lada Riva 1600SLX
- There's a three-month waiting list for a loaf of bread (five months if you want it ready-sliced)
- Cossack dancing looks stupid when done to a smoochy number
- Cossack dancing looks stupid *per se*

- A pair of holed, wee-stained M&S own-brand jeans costs the equivalent of a light aircraft
- Even a Big Mac in the Moscow McDonald's costs £84,000
- All Russian men look like Dennis Healey
- All Russian women look like Russian men
- On the four days of the year when the temperature gets above zero everyone is out in the parks, sunbathing in bikinis
- If you visit a Russian family it's traditional for them to offer you the best food in the house. Rat on a stick, yum, yum
- There are only seven shops in the whole of Moscow. Five of them are empty, one sells only turnips (Turnips R Us, 24 Red Square) and the seventh sells food but has a queue outside stretching back as far as the Ukraine, especially on days when the new Marmite jar is put on display
- Their album chart contains 24 different balalaika collections

SADDAM HUSSEIN — model yourself on this great man by adopting his hobbies . . . !

- Torture
- International terrorism
- Sneaking a quick one off the wrist in between council of war meetings
- Trying to imitate his idol, Mike Morris
- Dressing up in women's clothing and looking for Iraqi soldiers on leave
- Sneaking up behind young goatherds and slipping it to them
- Whining incessantly about how evil it is if anyone retaliates against your crackpot murderous schemes
- Nerve gas your own people deliberately and then condemn America for accidentally killing a few civilians
- Sleep with your mother whenever possible
- Or your father, depending on who isn't busy with the sheep that night
- Stand in front of the mirror for hours, adjusting your beret and thinking how much like Tom

Selleck you look — also while having one off the wrist

- Keep pin-ups of Sylvester Stallone, Mike Tyson and Rin-Tin-Tin in your war room
- Murder lots of innocent Arabs and fellow Muslims and then declare yourself the champion of the Arab world and of Islam . . .

SALVATION ARMY — why they're useless

- They carry tambourines instead of Armalites
- Where were they during the Gulf War when we needed them?
- They were also conspicuous by their absence at Goose Green in the Falklands, leaving 3 Para to do more than their fair share of the fighting
- You can't stop an advancing T54 with a clarinet
- They always gather in a tight formation, making them easy targets for a well-aimed mortar round
- Their lockers contain pin-ups of Cliff Richard and William Booth, not Arnold Schwarzenegger and Kim Basinger
- No one from their army has ever gone on to serve in the SAS
- Marching bands might frighten off Satan but are fairly ineffectual against crack Russian Spetznaz units
- There's nothing in the Bible to teach them 15 ways to kill a man with their bare hands (but there is lots about turning the other cheek — not a recommended move in hand-to-hand fighting)

SAMARITANS — politically incorrect and tactless phrases they should use to get rid of callers

- 'That's *your* problem . . .'
- 'Have you heard of EXIT?'

- 'So . . .?'
- 'Yes, actually 3 a.m. *is* a really inconvenient time to call'
- 'How the hell should I know?'
- 'I'm busy. Call me back in the morning'
- 'Tough shit'
- 'Does the term "loser" mean anything?'
- 'I don't blame her'
- 'Stop blubbing, you big cry baby!'

SCABS — why it's good to be an industrial scab

- You can flick V-signs at furious demonstrators as you sweep past them in a heavily protected police convoy
- You get to stick your bare bum out of the window at furious demonstrators as you sweep past them in a heavily protected police convoy
- You can shout witticisms like 'It'll never get better if you picket' out of the bus window
- You're helping to keep British industry going
- You can specialise in being a 'flying scab' — and enjoy a lot of variety in your work
- It's good to know the government appreciate your efforts
- You get to wreck people's entire lives — not an opportunity that arises all that often
- How else are you ever going to get a job?

SCHOOL — how to be one of the hard lads instead of the wimps

Wimps	*Hard lads*
Do their homework	Do kids for doing their homework
Look at insects under magnifying glasses	Put insects under magnifying glasses — and roast them
Regularly visit their	Regularly visit someone

granny	else's granny — and nick stuff
Collect stamps of the British Commonwealth	Collect slow-worms — which they then swallow for a dare in double physics
Play with Dinky cars	Play with high-performance XR3is nicked from the multi-storey
Spend ages making Airfix kits	Spend several seconds stamping on them after the wimps have made them
Know the Green Cross Code	Know how to fiddle the cashpoint machine
Always remember Father's Day	Spend Father's Day wondering
Score high on IQ tests	Get their name wrong on the paper
Go on holiday with their parents to the Dordogne	Go wherever the Variety Club of Great Britain take them
Play football with their friends	Play football with their pets
Have a larger collection of train numbers than anyone they know	Have a larger collection of pornography than the Vatican
Enjoy playing with kites	Enjoy being high as a kite
Pooh-pooh school dinners	Pooh-pooh during school dinners — and get referred to the school psychologist
Cross roads with the lollipop lady	Run back and forth across the road, giving the lollipop lady the finger
Eat their packed lunch	Eat someone else's

	packed lunch
Knock up a great balsa wood battleship	Knock up a girl in the third year
Get taken into university	Get taken into care
Grow up to work in banks	Grow up to blag them

SCHOOLS — where league tables will eventually lead us to

- They'll inevitably result in huge transfer fees being offered for the brightest pupils. Entire school budgets will disappear just to buy Caroline Finlay or Timothy Clarke (who might then tragically be off sick and be unable to perform during their GCSEs)
- Big businessmen like Alan Sugar will buy the school — only to sack the headmaster who made the school the success it was in the first place
- Successful schools will get millions in sponsorship money from big businesses who want their names on the back of pupils' blazers
- The most successful school in the borough will get to ride around in an open-top bus, waving their GCSE certificates to a cheering crowd
- Fanzines for schools will spring up like *When Monday Comes*
- Exams will become highly charged public spectacles held in front of capacity crowds with chants of 'Come on, you fifth years' and abuse for the adjudicator with chants like 'Who's that wanker in the corduroy!'
- Bob Holness will take over Brian Coleman's job as commentator for these events
- Teamwork will be discouraged (as it constitutes cheating) — but passing will be encouraged

- Sky TV will buy the rights to show live exams on their new Sky Euro Education 1 channel
- Instead of getting your results in the post, they will be revealed on *News at Ten*. Trevor McDonald will warn you to look away now if you don't want to see the final scores
- Instead of Saint and Greavesie, Magnus Magnusson and Bamber Gascoigne (Magnus and Bambi) will provide their own inimitable style of commentary

ALBERT SCHWEITZER — 10 dark secrets from the medical hero of the dark continent

- Albert Schweitzer was originally called Nobby Muller, but changed his name to sound like a nicer bloke
- Originally an academic musician, Schweitzer got into medicine completely by accident, when he told a Christian missionary that he had a particular interest in organs
- Schweitzer got into traction completely by accident by telling another churchman that he admired his organ and couldn't wait to get his hands on it
- Schweitzer had both a private and a public African practice. The rich tribal leaders got a genuine hypodermic full of anaesthetic. Poorer people had to settle for a placebo spear up the jacksie
- When visiting patients with leprosy, he would often exclaim 'Yuk!', barf up and then have to pretend it was a traditional German method of greeting
- If you tried to reach his paging service on the drums, he was never available
- Schweitzer said he founded his philosophy on a 'reverence for life — particularly if it was 36–23–36 and unmarried'

SCOTS — what they've contributed to world culture

- The incomprehensible poetry of Robbie Burns
- The incomprehensible accent of the average Scottish football player
- Clan treachery and deceit
- Ginger hair
- Men in skirts
- The Sporran — whatever that is
- The head butt
- The lyrically rewarding song 'Donald, Where's Yoor Troosers?'
- Several dozen unique excuses for not lending you any money
- The yummy haggis
- 'Scotty' from *Star Trek* (who wasn't really Scottish at all)

SECRET POLICE — why they do a good job

- Everyone likes surprises
- If you haven't done anything wrong there's nothing to worry about (if you're lucky)
- Without them, informants would have nothing to do
- If they weren't secret they wouldn't catch anybody
- It's exciting to be woken at 3 a.m. and bundled into the back of a waiting car
- They're a better way of showing disapproval with journalists than the Press Complaints Committee
- They're professionals and know when to stop torturing someone
- Without them, human-rights organisations would be twiddling their thumbs all day

SELLAFIELD — some public amenities that are a waste of money in the area

- Street lighting (everything glows at night anyway)
- A post office to hand out old age pensions
- The Sellafield Tourist Board
- All the signs saying 'Welcome to Sellafield. Twin town Chernobyl'
- The annual 'Let's Keep Sellafield Beautiful' festival
- The local job centre (there are always new vacancies at the plant)
- Incentive schemes to draw new companies to the area

SERIAL KILLERS — why it's good to be one

- You get to travel and meet people
- You don't have to worry about having a motive
- It's nice to read about yourself in the papers
- If you're caught you can blame 'those voices in your head' and escape a long prison sentence
- You are given a neat nickname by the media like 'Peter the Brain Eater' or the 'Suburban Slasher'
- You've got an outlet for your sexual inadequacies
- It's one of the few occupations where you get the chance to write a note taunting the police
- It's nice to know that your disturbed childhood finally amounted to something

SETI (THE SEARCH FOR EXTRA-TERRESTRIAL INTELLIGENCE) – obscene and specist messages we should be beaming to other races in the galaxy with our radio telescopes

- Human race, we're first class
  Other species kiss our arse!

- Planet Earth is number one
  Other planets up the bum
- The Solar System is the best
  Complete shite are all the rest
- We're the humans from Sol III
  The greatest race in the galaxy
- Human beings are miracles
  You slimy scum have tentacles
- Our home world is the best place
  We wouldn't shit upon your race
- We bet you aliens look like pukes
  Come visit us and we'll use our nukes
- There is other life in outer space
  And we're going to put you in your place
- Into deep space our signal delves
  With one clear message: go fuck yourselves
- Our planet is green and blue
  Yours probably looks like pooh
- We're the boys from Planet Earth
  And we're worth ten of what you're worth

SEX EDUCATION – politically incorrect ways to teach the facts of life at school

- Let the class watch you and one of the other teachers doing it in front of them
- Organise a school trip to a live sex show
- Or your town's red-light area (don't forget the parental consent form)
- Play a porno video
- Demonstrate using two rabbits from the biology lab, one of which is wearing a basque and suspenders
- Read out all the grafitti found on the toilet walls
- Demonstrate it yourself using an appropriate battery-operated sex aid
- Or the school dog
- Always advise against the use of condoms 'because they spoil the experience'

SEXISM — some good old sexist practices that need to make a comeback

- Wolf-whistling
- Pinching girls' bums
- Slapping girls' bums
- Telling any bird who won't sleep with you that she's frigid
- Letting her be responsible for birth control once more
- Serious kerb crawling
- Not taking 'no' for an answer
- Putting pin-ups on the office or factory wall

SEXUAL DESIRE — dubious terms for women with sexual desires

- Nymphos
- Slags
- Mattresses
- Slappers
- Bikes
- Easy
- The local sperm bank
- Bucket
- Open all hours
- Gagging for it
- Tarts
- Cheap
- Sluts

SEXUAL DESIRE — supposedly equally dubious terms for men with sexual desires

- Studs
- Lads
- That's about it, really . . .

SEXUAL FULFILMENT — why women should be denied it

- It's a bloody effort
- It's degrading for men to feel they have to perform
- Do it once and they'll expect it all the time
- It's too complex and difficult to accomplish after

eight pints and a nail-biting soccer match on the TV
- They can have more orgasms than a man — which is not fair and shouldn't be tolerated
- Treat 'em mean and keep 'em keen
- They'll start believing all the other crap in *Cosmopolitan*
- Do you want them to find out what they've been missing all these years?

SEXUAL HARASSMENT — some good ways to upset your secretary

- Photocopy your privates, autograph them, and leave them in her in-tray
- Record gynaecologically impossible suggestions on your dictaphone
- Pour Tipp-Ex down your trousers. Hide the bottle then corner your secretary and say, 'You're so horny, just look what you've made me do'
- Give her the kiss of life until she manages to knee you in that tender spot. Tell her you heard this was the typing pool and you thought she was drowning
- Walk up to her holding a large card postal tube to your groin and wink knowingly
- If she asks to borrow your Pritt, unzip your flies and show her everything you've got. When she looks aghast say that you misheard her
- Offer to give her a bikini-line waxing with the masking tape you pinched from the despatch department

SHOPLIFTING — its advantages

- It provides employment for store detectives
- You can dispense with queues
- You don't have to face a dopey shop assistant who can't work the new till

- You avoid any chance of getting in the 'six items or less' line by mistake
- Or being about to pay and finding you've left your wallet at home
- You know what 3 lb of prime pork down your trouser leg feels like for the first time in your life
- You don't need to worry about having a £1 coin for the trolley
- Or getting one with a wobbly wheel
- Inflation is irrelevant

SHORT PEOPLE — why 'people of diminutive stature' are a pain in the arse

- They're always asking you to reach something on a shelf for them
- They're hard to see if you're meeting them in a crowded place
- They tend to marry short people and therefore perpetuate the genetic flaw
- You can never look them in the eye to know what they're thinking
- They can get into the cinema cheaper than you
- If you want to punch them in the bollocks you have to really crouch down
- They, however, have no problem in giving you a really nasty bite in the bollocks in return
- They think there's some sort of prejudice against them by people of average, or above average height
- They're right

SICKNESS AND INVALIDITY BENEFITS — exclusive! Ingenious new schemes to save us all money on claims!

- All wheelchair ramps should be removed from DSS buildings

- If a man has one arm and therefore 75 per cent of his limbs, it follows that he should only receive 75 per cent of sickness benefits. People with further limbs missing will require less benefit in proportion
- DSS offices should be moved every week to confuse the registered blind
- Those suffering from ME or any other form of severe fatigue should be allocated to the longest queue
- People suffering from chronic arthritis in the hands shall be made to complete, in their own handwriting, a 1,476-page declaration prior to having their claim assessed
- Files will be misplaced behind radiators or in skips whenever possible
- Claimants with Parkinson's Disease should be told that their shaking is indicative of guilty feelings and have their claims suspended indefinitely, pending an investigation
- People who are too sick to attend the DSS offices will be conveniently forgotten about
- NHS treatment will be scaled down to allow further attrition on those claiming sickness benefit

SKINNY PEOPLE — why they should be ruthlessly persecuted

- They make the rest of us feel like Nellie the fucking Elephant
- People think they must be movie stars or models
- They say things like 'I can eat 109,000 giant-sized Mars bars — and not put on an ounce. Isn't it amazing?'
- They're the only ones who can wear fashionable designer clothes
- They're the only people who look good in jeans
- Ever been about to take a really big juicy bite

into a Big Mac when someone slender and
svelte walked past your table?
- They are indirectly responsible for hundreds of
thousands of us drinking revolting diet
milkshakes every day
- Because they're so weedy they're easy to duff up

SLAUGHTERHOUSES — why it's good to work in one

- You can take out your grudge against cattle and
there's nothing they can do about it
- The animals are trussed up and helpless — so
it's a nice safe occupation
- You can easily make yourself the company
comedian by coming out with cracks like
'Squeek, Piggie, Squeek!' or 'Cop this,
Daisybell!'
- You can pretend you're a ruthless serial killer
- Sometimes the stunning process doesn't work
and you have to leap into action with your
butchering gear immediately
- When bores ask you what you do at a party, you
can say you work in an abattoir — that usually
shuts them up
- It's safer than working for the Serbs in Bosnia —
and just as satisfying
- You can bring intestines home with you and
chase the wife around the house with them for
a giggle
- You may be invited onto *Bruce Forsyth's
Generation Game* to imitate the screams of dying
animals for contestants to copy
- As long as people don't realise what goes on in
slaughterhouses, there'll always be a demand
for meat and you're sure of a job for life

189

SLAVERY — why it should be reintroduced

- Just for the hell of it
- It would give us something to do with the Welsh
- No one's written a decent spiritual since the 1860s
- It would be good to have a new form of trade that Britain traditionally excels at
- While everyone's up in arms about the reintroduction of slavery, the government can do what they want to the NHS and no one will care
- You'd never have to wash behind the cooker again in your life
- It could be called a government training scheme and used as a way of reducing the dole queues
- It would be a very neat way of side-stepping the European Social Charter

SLUMS — why we need them

- They make even the average bits of a city look wonderful
- Without them where would the poor people live?
- To make us all grateful we're not there
- Without slums people wouldn't be able to forage for food or clothes amongst the rubbish
- Mosquitos and rats have got to breed somewhere

SOAP OPERAS — more politically correct names for your TV favourites

- *Community Participants (Neighbours)*
- *Emmerdale Livestock Concentration Camp (Emmerdale Farm)*
- *Renewal of Reactionary Monarchistic Regime Street (Coronation Street)*
- *Parental Responsibilities (Sons and Daughters)*
- *Expatriate Britons with Colonial, Post-*

*Imperialist Attitudes and Negative Thespian
Qualities (Eldorado)*
- *Proletarians (EastEnders)*
- *Nepotistic Time-Spanning Structure of Wealth
  and Power Perpetuation (Dynasty)*
- *The Pigs (The Bill)*
- *Liberty-deprived, Circumferentially Challenged
  Non-Heterosexuals of Cell Block H (Prisoners
  of Cell Block H)*

SOLAR POWER — why it's useless

- It doesn't work at night
- On a typically grimy British day, the average
  solar generator produces enough energy to
  power an egg whisk
- Everyone knows the sun causes cancer, so how
  can we be sure that solar power is safe? We
  might all get melanomas from just sitting under
  a solar-powered light bulb
- When the sun goes behind a cloud, an entire city
  might suffer a devastating power cut
- The sun is more powerful than a million billion
  atom bombs — but we're told atomic power
  isn't safe
- In the winter, the sun's at its weakest just when
  we most need power for heating and lighting

SOLDIERS — why women are no good in the army

- They want to use Jiff and Mr Sheen to clean
  their rifles
- They won't be able to obey the order 'Stand by
  your beds' as they'll be too busy making them
- They'll always be late for battles
- They can't keep an ordinary secret, let alone a
  military one

191

- Lip gloss will make them visible to the enemy at 500 yards
- They'll spend hours trying to choose the right shade of green for camouflage
- They're always disappointed when they find out that a battle dress actually consists of combat trousers
- They burst into tears whenever a commanding officer shouts at them
- They're afraid to dig a trench in case they break their nails
- You can't rub shoe polish over their bollocks as part of an army initiation ceremony

SONGS — how the politically correct brigade would retitle our favourite songs if they got their hands on them

- 'Emotionally Well-Developed, Non-Adult Person Towards Whom I Have an Unhealthy Possessive Attitude' — Guns 'N' Roses ('Sweet Child of Mine')
- 'World War Two Pilot Who Terminally Inconvenienced At Least Five Non-Mutual Pilots, with Melanin Enriched Characteristics' — Motorhead ('Ace of Spades')
- 'My Male Phallic Repressive Organ' — Chuck Berry ('My Ding-A-Ling')
- 'Undergone the Birthing Experience with Accompanying Trauma Only to Develop Modes and Customs Deemed Unacceptable by Society' — Steppenwolf ('Born to be Wild')
- 'Non-Sexually Specific Object with Strong Naturistic Tendencies' — The Troggs ('Wild Thing')
- 'The Academically Challenged Person on the Hill' — The Beatles ('The Fool on the Hill')
- 'It's Precipitating Persons of the Male Gender' — The Weather Girls ('It's Raining Men')

192

- 'Melanin Favoured and Melanin Deprived' — Paul McCartney and Stevie Wonder ('Ebony and Ivory')
- 'I Believe, in My Typically Heterosexualist Male Way, that I Have Possessive Rights Over This Particular Person of Female Gender' — Paul McCartney and Michael Jackson ('The Girl is Mine')
- 'Posterially Challenged Persons of the Female Gender' — Queen ('Fat-bottomed Girls')
- 'She Wears Indigenous Ethnic Apparel' — Guy Mitchell ('She Wears Red Feathers and a Hooly-Hooly Skirt')
- 'Female Parent, Your Offspring Are All Emotionally Challenged at Present' — Slade ('Mama, We're All Crazee Now')

SOUL — proof that the human soul does not exist

- Bob Monkhouse

SOUP KITCHENS — why it's not good to eat in them

- You get loads of tramps there
- The décor is basic and the ambience almost non-existent
- You can't book a table and there's always a queue to get in
- There's very little choice (it's always the *soupe du jour*)
- There's no wine list, just a mug of tea
- It's not suitable for impressing a girl on a first date
- It's hard to enjoy your meal when everyone around you is comparing their boils
- They do require you to wear a tie — but it's round your waist
- If you get your wallet out at the end and offer to

pay, 14 vagabonds will wrestle you to the
ground and give you a good kicking

SOUTH AMERICA — what it's good for

- Inflation at 6,000 per cent
- Death squads
- Political leaders so corrupt that they make
  Robert Maxwell look like Matthew Corbett
- Putting 10,000 volts through the genitals of
  political prisoners
- Displacing whole tribes of Amazonian Indians
- Providing safe havens for drug barons
- And ex-Nazis
- Destroying the rain forest at the rate of 100 acres
  a minute
- Keeping Amnesty International busy
- Avoiding

SOUTHERNERS — some reet champion reasons
to hate 'em

- 'Cos they're Southerners
- They're soft, man
- Aye, an' toffee-nosed with it
- Aye, an' half of 'em don't know they're born
- They think they're God's gift 'cos they've got a
  job and a home
- They drink cold beer
- They've never tasted proper fish and chips nor
  scampi in a basket in their lives
- Winter? They don't know what winter is!
- Just because they've got indoor privies they
  think they're Jesus Christ Almighty

SPACE EXPLORATION — why it's better to spend
money on this than feeding the starving

- The starving won't enable us to push back the
  frontiers of science

- The money spent on rockets might enable us to find another planet with loads of spare food that we can harvest
- Alternatively, it might enable us to send all the starving people into orbit
- Watching a multi-million-dollar Saturn 5 leave the launch pad is more exciting than watching a person slowly starve
- The Space Shuttle is reusable — three tons of grain are not
- It's hard to imagine a world without Teflon-coated frying pans and LCD watches, just two of the valuable spin-offs from space technology
- It was only by spending billions and billions of dollars that scientists were able to disprove that the moon was not, after all, made of green cheese (as the starving had hoped)
- Or that Mars was not a planet made of caramel and chocolate 4,200 miles in diameter
- Rocket scientist is a much more dynamic-sounding career than nutritionist
- It's far more dangerous to supply food to Somalia than go up in a space shuttle

SPANISH ETHNIC GROUPS — some particularly stupid-sounding ones

- The Basques
- The Corsets
- The Girdles
- The Bolsters
- The Halter Tops
- The Nighties
- The Teddies
- The Lingerie
- The Suspendies
- The Frilly Garters
- The Undies
- The Peek-A-Boo Bras
- The Crotchless Panties

SPECIESISM — why it's necessary to discriminate between animals

- Dog and chips doesn't sound very appetising
- You won't get very far in a coach pulled by lobsters
- A guard ant is useless, to all intents and purposes
- A guide rattlesnake does not inspire confidence or trust in the blind
- Cockroach milk would lead to a flood of cancelled orders for Unigate
- A panther is not a suitable first pet for a child
- The Grand National will never be won by a hippo, regardless of the jockey

SPECIESISM — why it's necessary to discriminate *in favour* of animals over humans at times

- The Royal Coach wouldn't be nearly so impressive — nor so fast — if it was pulled by four courtiers
- People wouldn't stand for experimental cosmetics being squirted in other people's eyes
- No one wants to eat people — not even Andes plane-crash survivors
- The next time you visit Weston-super-Mare, consider how much demand there would be for 'people rides'
- The traditional 'Christmas Human' has an unappetising ring about it
- No human will willingly go and live with some unhappy and lonely old 70-year-old
- You can't tie fireworks to humans' tails
- Battery humans would be uncivilised — and unproductive
- A sign on your gate saying 'Beware of the Human' is meaningless

SPEED LIMIT — reasons for raising it to 100 mph

- Sales reps would be able to make more calls per day therefore helping to stimulate the economy
- We'd all get through more petrol, thus enabling us to collect loads more Esso tokens
- If you did break down because your car was worn out you wouldn't have to wait so long for the AA or RAC because they could travel to you faster
- We could afford to leave slightly later (or even have a lie-in) and still get to our destinations on time
- Cars would wear out that much quicker, forcing us to buy new ones and therefore helping the depressed car industry
- Ambulances would be able to reach the scene of an accident quicker
- It wouldn't take so long to reach the next service station for a slash
- We could have races with other cars at speeds of up to 100 mph and *still be within the speed limit!!!*
- There would be far more donor organs available for people who desperately need transplants . . .

STATUES — and other displays we should erect in London to upset foreigners

- A 30-foot bronze statue of 'Bomber' Harris doing a Moonie outside the German Embassy
- . . . right next to the 100-foot statue of Geoff Hurst
- A statue of Salman Rushdie reading from *The Satanic Verses* outside the Iranian Embassy — if there is one this week
- A large statue of Ho Chi Minh giving the finger outside the US Embassy in Grosvenor Square
- A statue of General de Gaulle enjoying sex with

a chicken, strategically positioned outside the French Embassy
- A statue of a naked woman drinking from a Scotch bottle outside the Saudi Consulate
- A scale replica of the *Belgrano*, placed where staff from the Argentinian Embassy cannot help but see it
- A full-sized replica of a whale with a harpoon through it, right outside the Norwegian Embassy
- A giant fluorescent billboard opposite the Japanese Embassy that flashes the legend 'Enola Gay' again and again and again and again . . .
- A big statue of Richard Burton doing unmentionable things to Dylan Thomas with a large leek — just to offend unwelcome Welsh visitors on cheap Awaydays

STING — if the rain forest is so bloody good, why doesn't he live there?

- He's frightened of spiders
- A primitive people whose only form of musical expression is banging two sticks together and gibbering cannot possibly appreciate the musical genius behind 'De Do Do Do, De Da Da Da'
- No one would ask for his autograph (they don't have any concept of the written language)
- It's a seven-day steamboat ride up the Limpopo to the nearest store selling peroxide
- With his blond hair and white skin he stands out like a sore thumb and is an easy target for blow-pipe pranksters
- He's probably frightened of getting his head shrunk (at least it would then match the amount of hair he has)
- There's no tax advantage (you have to give 50 per cent of all your wealth to the local chief)

- Stuart Copeland once came to visit him and got swallowed by an anaconda

STING – 14 ideologically unsound songs that he should sing

- 'The Lumberjack's Song'
- 'Fat Bottomed Girls'
- 'Street Fighting Man'
- 'Nice Legs, Shame About the Face'
- 'Do Ya Think I'm Sexy?'
- 'So Macho'
- 'Shaddap Your Face'
- 'Small People (Got No Reason to Live)'
- 'If I Said You Had A Beautiful Body Would You Hold It Against Me?'
- 'Tobacco Road'
- 'Itsy Bitsy Teeny Weeny Yellow Polka Dot Bikini'
- 'Money Money Money'
- 'Get Outta My Dreams Get Into My Car'
- 'Some Girls Will (Some Girls Won't . . .)'

STONEHENGE — why we should tear it down

- It's old
- It looks untidy
- We have far more efficient lunar and solar calendars these days
- It will piss off the Druids and the hippies
- Everybody who sees it thinks it's no big deal anyway
- If it really was built by an alien intelligence, the act will be a clear V sign flicked at the stars
- The demolition work will give valuable new jobs to the construction industry
- We could use the land to build Sega World in its place
- The Americans might buy it

- Do we need it? Be honest now, imagine you're having a ruthless spring clean. Would you keep Stonehenge or would you chuck it?

SUPER-TANKER CAPTAINS — why those who run aground should not be prosecuted

- They didn't do it on purpose
- Have you ever tried steering a super-tanker?
- You'd be an alki as well if you were stuck at sea for three months at a time with only a selection of *Inspector Morse* videos and a Sonia LP to break the monotony and a surly crew who only spoke Liberian
- You don't prosecute someone whose car leaks a little oil, do you?
- What do a few seagulls and otters matter?
- Those maps would confuse *anyone*
- Will putting them in prison clear up the mess?

SACKED SUPER-TANKER CAPTAINS — things you shouldn't trust them with

- Driving a Eurojuggernaut
- Driving a Reliant Robin
- Demonstrating your toy company's new remote-controlled boat
- Looking after the paddleboat concession at the local lido
- Towing you while you water-ski
- Not to piss in their own bathwater
- Being lighthouse keepers
- Anything that makes them responsible for chemicals in any quantity whatsoever
- Anything that requires a sense of direction
- Anything that requires a degree of sobriety

SWEARING — why it's good

- Because it fucking well is
- It's impressive to prove that you know 20 different names for the genitalia
- It's more civilised to swear at someone than punch them in the face — and marginally safer, too
- It's the only chance you get to describe someone as looking like the female sexual organs
- You can do it to anyone, anywhere
- Anything that widens your vocabulary shouldn't be dismissed out of hand
- It makes you feel grown up
- There's nothing else to do on the back of a night bus
- It's the only language Dixon's customer complaints department understands
- *Viz* does it all the time and it's the most popular magazine going

TALES OF THE RIVER BANK — **some adventures Hammy and Ratty would enjoy if the series was made today**

- Hammy innocently drinks some yellow sludge floating on the surface of the river and grows to 70 feet tall. This is probably not the best time to go and visit his cousin Dougal in London . . .
- Hammy is trying to sell his burrow — but none of the other animals want to live by the riverside . . .
- Sewage surfing. Shit's up! The latest craze for the riverside animals is sewage surfing — complete with pseudo Beach Boys soundtrack
- Vince Vole moves into his new home — a sewage outlet pipe. He finds it difficult to make friends amongst the riverside folk except Hammy, who has a bad cold. When Hammy's nose clears, he soon buggers off . . .
- Oh dear! The military have dumped some test chemicals by the Riverbank and all the animals are on a huge LSD trip . . . man
- Times are hard. Chemicals have killed off all the food on the Riverbank . . . and Hammy's

starting to look remarkably succulent to
Roderick
- When a toxic spill causes Hammy to glow in the
dark, Ratty is terrified he is a ghost
- It's the night of a full moon. Roderick is
beginning to turn into a wererat . . . or is it
rabies?
- There goes the neighbourhood. Wally Weasel has
moved into the riverbank and is rapidly eating
his way through the indigenous population . . .

TATTOOS — forehead tattoos, how to choose the right one

Suitable forehead tattoos	Unsuitable forehead tattoos
mental	arsehole
NF skins	4th Harrow Venture Scouts
HATE	melancholy
vicious	ticklish
Hitler	Sting
tough	big old softie
Fascist	Tory wet
psychopath	borderline schizophrenic
killer	advertising executive
punk	the big band sound
Sid Vicious	Syd Lawrence
Charles Manson	Charles Dance
Satan	Snoopy
big cock	big prick
hard	detumescent
death	taxes
fuck you!	coo-eee!
Borstal boy	wet play monitor

TEACHERS — why it's good for students to have affairs with them

- You get to see each other every day of the week
- You'll automatically get good marks for essays
- You can blackmail them for even better marks
- You can get a lift to and from school
- You've automatically got a date for the school disco
- Your parents are pleased you're dating someone with a good, steady job
- You hear all the dirt on the other teachers
- You won't mind getting detention
- When it's open evening your parents get the chance to informally meet their potential future son or daughter-in-law
- Older partners have a wealth of experience to share — and a more mature attitude towards contraception than fellow pupils

TEENAGE PREGNANCIES — why they're good

- You can be a grandmother when you're 32 and win all the Glamorous Granny contests hands down
- While you're in labour you don't need to do any homework
- You can use Child Benefit to supplement your pocket money
- You can prove, once and for all, to everyone at school that you've actually 'done it'
- You can have cravings for crisps, chocolate and hamburgers and not worry — that's what you eat anyway
- You can get out of any difficult exam by pretending you're going into labour and being rushed to hospital
- You can get out of wearing school uniform and doing gym

- Because you live at home your mum can babysit for you every single night of the week
- Any time you're late for class you can blame it on being up all night feeding the baby
- You no longer need to worry about *getting* pregnant

TELEVISION — politically unsound shows to be broadcast in Turkey

- The 'Sexypants the Sheep' Show
- Buttock Squad!
- The Little Leather Cherubs Song and Dance Spectacular
- Shepherd at Large
- Have Vaseline, Will Travel
- Celebrity Reacharound
- Oh, You Wicked Moustachioed Muscleman Dreamboat You!
- Mustapha's Mule
- One Man and His Dog
- Whose Botty?

TERMINAL ILLNESSES — politically incorrect ways that doctors should break the news to you

- A singing telegram delivered by someone dressed as a clown
- Via a game of charades
- On a banner towed behind a light aircraft flying over your house
- Written in icing on a special cake presented to you in the surgery
- A letter read out live on the radio by Simon Bates
- Flyposted on a vacant shop near where you live
- In a game of hangman played in the surgery
- By wearing a black cloth over his head as soon as you enter his office

- Shouting it at you through a megaphone
- By pretending he's got some really good news for you and inviting you down to the surgery

MRS THATCHER — why we should bring her back

- Things couldn't be any worse

THEATRE — politically incorrect ideas for West End spectaculars

- *Spank Me, Gandhi!*
- *Douglas Bader — The Ballet*
- *Helen Keller — The Musical* (featuring the smash-hit song 'Nyuh, Nyuh, Hyuh')
- *O Calcutta!* (an all-nude version of the Mother Theresa Story)
- *Ooh, La La, Hiroshima!*
- *The Elephant Man on Ice*
- *Mosley!* — a good old-fashioned East End knees-up (between the legs)

THEATRES — why they should all be shut down

- Plays are boring and nowhere near as good as films
- You can't smoke in the theatre
- Ticket prices are extortionate
- It would serve Andrew Lloyd-Webber right for being such a smartarse
- So we'd lose *Starlight Express* — hardly the end of civilisation as we know it
- People get cross if you chomp popcorn all the way through the first act
- People get angry if you have a good natter for 20 minutes in a theatre like you can in a cinema
- Everybody knows it was the policeman who did it in *The Mousetrap* now
- You never see stars like Bruce Willis or Big Arnie

treading the boards; only second-rate English
actors who can't make it in Hollywood
- Half-time bar drinks cost twice as much as the
tickets – and it takes twice as long as the first
half to actually get served

THIRD WORLD — what it's good for

- Blue Peter appeals
- Expendable, cheap labour in dangerous foreign
chemical plants
- Buying obsolete Western jet fighters
- Exploitation of minerals on a major scale
- TV news reports to tug at our heart strings
- Families so large that they must bring in a
fortune in Child Benefit
- Leaders with funny names and even funnier
headgear
- Dumping grounds for American
pharmaceuticals that have already been
withdrawn from sale on the home market
- An untapped market for Western cigarette
manufacturers
- Soaking up Western aid like there's no tomorrow
(which, in fact, there won't be . . .)

THE THIRD WORLD DEBT — why they should be made to pay it off

- They owe it to us
- When was the last time your bank let you off a
fiver, let alone a few hundred billion dollars?
- If they have the funds to pay for secret nuclear
arms research, they can afford to make a few
repayments now and again
- Maybe if they didn't insist on having such big
armies, they might be able to pay their bills
- If we got the money back, it would end our
recession overnight

- We generated that wealth through our hard work; they were too busy starving or clearing up after some natural disaster to get on their bikes and do some grafting

THE THIRD WORLD DEBT — excuses they make not to pay it back

- Oh. We didn't get your letter
- Sorry, we had a cyclone this month
- The cheque's in the post — but unfortunately we don't have a postal service here
- We had the money, but then we had a bloody civil war and we had to spend it all on napalm and T-72s . . .
- Lend us some more dosh and we'll pay you back out of that. Honest
- Tell you what; double or quits . . .
- I'm sorry, el Presidente's out at the moment. Would you like to leave a message?
- We're offsetting the debt against the hundreds of years of colonial exploitation, wealth stripping and slavery you inflicted on us. In other words, bog off, white man . . .

THE THIRD WORLD DEBT — some positive steps to get our money back

- Write them a stern bank letter — and charge them for it too!
- Send the boys round to break a few fingers
- Repossess their countries
- Seize their assets. (We could have a special 'hovel' auction)
- Put them on a 'credit blacklist' so they can't get any more tanks and warplanes on tick . . .
- Seize all the goods they export to us, then refuse to pay for them and tell them they're being offset against the debt

- Threaten the entire Third World with a jail sentence if they default. (This might not work, however, because at least you're guaranteed three meals a day and a roof over your head in prison)
- Buy more cocaine — that way, Third World countries might be able to pay off their debts one day

TOBACCO COMPANIES — more politically incorrect things for them to sponsor instead of healthy sporting events

- The Sellafield Reprocessing Centre
- The El Salvadorian Death Squads
- Lung-transplant clinics
- The vultures at Whipsnade Zoo
- The toxic waste trains that pass through your local station when you're asleep
- Periodic flu epidemics
- The M25
- Jeffrey Archer novels

(If the cigarette companies do insist on continuing to fund sports events, for the sake of integrity they should limit themselves to only certain sports — like freefall bungee jumping and Russian roulette.)

TONGUE WAGGLING — what men really mean when they employ this seemingly politically incorrect gesture

- 'I would like to date you'
- 'All this could be yours if you would only consent to be my fiancée'
- 'Don't think I haven't noticed you over there in the corner, you perky little minx'
- 'Ha! You think I'm a hopeless inadequate and won't spare me the time of day — but I have

all the necessary equipment for your satisfaction!'
- 'Excuse me, miss, but I find you too attractive for mere words'
- 'How can I be a virgin if I know how to do this?'
- 'Good evening, barmaid'
- 'I think your girlfriend should be with me, rather than you, my good fellow'

TORIES — how we can ensure they are returned to office again

- Black magic
- Pass a law making it a hanging offence to vote for anyone else
- A bloody *coup d'état*
- Only giving the vote to committed mental patients
- Rigging the ballot on a national scale
- Getting them to apologise for everything and promising to try harder in future. (It worked at the last election)

TOURETTE'S SYNDROME — suitable occupations for sufferers

- Doctors' receptionists
- BR platform staff
- 'Dummy' pupils for trainee teachers
- Old-fashioned shoeshine boy
- Spitting for Britain in the annual tobacco-spitting championships
- The one who goes 'Pchhh Pchhh' in a rap posse
- The British Army
- Serious Roy Hattersley impersonators
- British National Party spokesmen

TOWER BLOCKS — why it's good to live in a council tower block

- You can look straight down birds' dresses
- You can spot the pigs coming a mile off
- You can gob down on to elderly residents
- You can drop heavy or filthy objects down on to elderly residents
- You can keep wrecking the lifts until the old people die of heart failure and your mates get to move in instead
- You've probably got a fence on the same floor as you
- You can go on TV and say that you do glue only because of your living conditions — and they'll believe you
- You get a great view of all the joyriders doing stunts around the estate — but you're high up enough not to become an accidental fatality
- If the bathroom's occupied you can piss out the window

TOY GUNS — why it's good for children to play with them

- It teaches them about the horror of warfare (either that, or the glory of warfare)
- They can't very well re-create the excitement of the Gulf War with a Weeble and an Etch-A-Sketch
- They help them identify with role models like Dirty Harry, Mark Chapman or Al Capone
- It's less harmful than buying them boxing gloves
- Or playing with *real* guns
- You're never too young to learn how to be a soldier of fortune
- If the children don't want to play with them, they won't
- It's good training for a career as a armed robber or police marksman

- It's character building

TRADITION — 10 good words to describe other people's cultures and traditions

- Barbaric
- Outdated
- Sad
- Incomprehensible
- Stinky
- Ridiculous
- Primitive
- Boring
- Worthless
- Shite

TRANSVESTITISM — why it should be stamped out completely

- It's unnatural and against God: no major biblical character is ever described as wearing lacy suspenders and a bra for any reason
- You might chat up a transvestite by mistake and invite them back home for a nightcap. *It happens . . .*
- It might breathe new life into 'ladies' nights'
- Men who indulge in it need special help, not special nightclubs
- It would completely fuck up Barry Humphries' career
- If men want to dress as women, they should go to Iran, where, in all-encompassing black robes, no one will be able to tell
- It would help 'some of us' to resist temptation
- There is absolutely *nothing* erotic about putting on your wife's soft, cool panties and bra and her slinkiest dress and then feeling the cool caress of nylon as you slide each stocking slowly and sensuously up your leg to be pinned to your French-style suspender belt. Nothing

TRIAL BY JURY — why it should be abolished

- Jurors can be intimidated by mean-looking defendants winking at them
- Some jury members make a trial last longer than it should just so they can get a free night in a hotel (with full English breakfast)
- You can't choose the type of case you want to sit through
- You have to stay awake during the whole case, even if it's a boring tax fraud
- Whole juries can be nobbled, necessitating an expensive re-trial
- There's not enough society sex scandals or gangland axe murders to go round
- It's not so much fun without the death penalty
- There's usually a fist fight over who gets to be the foreman of the jury
- Who needs a jury when you can tell if a person's guilty just by the way they look

TRIBAL PEOPLES — why they make life hard for themselves

- They make their medicines from bark and rare orchids when all they need do is walk into Boots
- Standing in front of Tesco's fish counter holding a £10 note is far easier than standing in front of a small stream holding a spear
- They walk around naked in jungles full of prickly plants and animals with sharp teeth
- They shove things that look like wooden CDs in their bottom lips and then wonder why they have difficulty making themselves understood
- They cut tribal markings into their faces when a school tie or blazer crest is far less painful
- They spend months in a 'menstruation hut' for

initiation into womanhood when they could
buy tampons in any supermarket
- If they're going to sit round a camp fire telling
the same tribal stories time after time they
might just as well be watching repeats on
television
- Their hut walls are full of drawings of animals
rather than posters of the latest pop idols
- The tribal men wrestle with dangerous beasts
and climb tall trees to prove their manliness
whereas all they need do is hold a drinking
contest and pull a bird

TRUANCY — why it doesn't matter

- The kids who play truant are the kids who won't
get any GCSEs if they were in school or not
- It's good practice for when kids can't get jobs
and have to hang around on street corners
- It teaches good skiving skills if they do manage
to get a job
- If they're playing truant they're not disrupting
the class for anyone else
- Or attacking the teacher
- Smaller classes are easier to manage
- Kids can learn loads of new skills on the streets
which will benefit them in later life, such as
windscreen cleaning and shoplifting

UNDERTAKERS — politically incorrect ways to behave in your job

- Play *Thunderbirds* puppets with the corpses
- Put all the male corpses in women's dresses — just to see the reaction of the relatives when they visit the Chapel of Rest
- Refer to the deceased as 'the stiff'
- Play Radio 1 in the Chapel of Rest instead of solemn Muzak; if relatives complain, tell them the dead don't care
- Turn up on the day of the funeral in a satanic goat's head and swirling red cloak and say, 'You were the family who wanted the black magic ceremony, weren't you?'
- Sneak into the bereaved's home at night and prop the body up in an armchair. Yell 'Honey I'm home!' as loud as you can and then scarper
- Sell the body to medical research and load the coffin with a clothing dummy and some bricks
- Get together with a rival undertaker and have a 'corpse boxing match'
- Charge the bereaved an outrageous sum of

money — they'll be too distraught to query your bill

THE UNEMPLOYED — why they're really jammy bastards

- They don't have to commute
- They get reduced admission to the local leisure centre
- They can watch *The Time, The Place* on TV in the mornings
- They don't have to take shit from the boss
- They can enjoy a nice peaceful nap in the afternoons
- They don't have to take work home with them
- They don't have to wake up to Derek Jameson in the morning
- They can go to matinées of movies and have the entire cinema to themselves
- They don't need a clean shirt every day
- They're especially jammy because the Conservatives won a fourth term in office — against all odds — allowing them to stay out of work

UNITED NATIONS — why it's a stupid idea

- Any old crap country can join
- They let fascists become their leaders with remarkable ease
- The Arab nations just use it as a base for terrorism, propaganda and generally making nuisances of themselves
- They can't do anything effective, in any situation, ever
- United Nations sanctions are about as effective as a condom designed to double as a cauliflower strainer

- Everybody hates everybody else in the United Nations, so they're hardly united
- Everyone knows that America runs the world, so why the pretence of democratic decision-making?
- How you can possibly respect an organisation led by a man called Boutros Boutros Ghali? What is this? Is he so good they named him twice? Did his dad stutter at the christening or what?

UNIVERSAL SUFFRAGE — why it was a bad idea

- John Major won the last election because women voters thought he was sexier than Neil Kinnock — which is pretty sad and doesn't bode well for John Smith in the future
- Women are more likely to deliberately vote Conservative anyway
- Working-class people are more likely to accidentally vote Conservative anyway
- Politicians have to appeal to the lowest common denominator to get elected
- When we get a shit government — which is nearly always — we can't point to the electorate and blame them — because we all had a chance to vote
- Universal suffrage is full of odd paradoxes — like loonies can't vote, but they can become Secretary of State for the Environment
- If Ian McShane ever becomes leader of a political party, all the women who fancy him will automatically put that party into power

UNSAFE SEX — why it's exciting

- You *know* you can beat the odds!

THE UNTOUCHABLES — why the Indian caste system is a brilliant idea

- You have a regular supply of people to do the shit jobs no one else wants to do without resorting to bringing in immigrants
- You can sneer and spit on the poor and you actually get religious brownie points for it
- Divinely inflicted poverty is a brilliant way of explaining social inequality
- 'The Untouchables' is an inspired name; it makes them sound filthy and loathsome, so you're not tempted to help them
- It also puts you off having sex with them and diluting or confusing the caste structure
- It's far better than our humble class system

UNWANTED CHILDREN — cruel ways to arrange adoptions

- Raffles
- Lucky dips
- Baby hoop-la
- Bobbing for babies in a barrel
- An auction for desperate childless couples
- Advertise in the local newspaper:

　　For sale: Girl aged 8 months. Potty-trained. Box 140

　　For sale: Baby boy. Will exchange for wok. Box 62

　　For sale: Baby boy (unwanted gift). Box 342

　　Bargain: Girl aged one month; will deliver. Box 12

　　Wanted: Good home (or even mediocre one, really) for little girl aged one next month. Box 17

URUGUAY — its best-selling items

- Forged passports and IDs
- German–Uruguayan dictionaries
- Wigs
- False moustaches (any style except black toothbrush)
- Tip-offs about the arrival of Simon Wiesenthal at the Montevideo International Airport
- Paintings that have been missing for 50 years
- Gold-smelting equipment
- Tattoo-removal cream
- *Odessa File* videos
- Diplomatic immunity

UTOPIA — why it can never exist, despite what the 'New Age' dreamers will have you believe

- People will always fuck each other over for a buck; it's human nature
- For thousands of years we've been heading in the opposite direction, so how could we change course now?
- Britain in the future will still include Milton Keynes
- Utopia implies equality for all — and there simply isn't enough to go round
- The last bunch who tried to create a Utopia succeeded in massacring millions of people and plunging the whole world into war
- It is impossible to have your cake and eat it. For example, in a Utopia you should be able to sleep with anyone you want to and yet at the same time refuse to sleep with anyone you don't want to. This is what we call an insoluble paradox. Shame, really . . .

VALIUM — the real reasons why doctors prescribe it

- To shut you up
- To ensure you go away happy
- So you can be 'one of the girls' with all your friends
- So they can call in the next nutjob and do precisely the same
- To stop you realising that they're doing nothing about your real problem
- To stop them having to make an expensive referral to the local psychiatric outpatients unit
- Because newer, safer drugs are more expensive
- To keep you so mellow you wouldn't dream of making a complaint
- Because they believe they're not responsible for society fucking you up in the first place
- Because they can't do anything about your marriage to a psychopath and your two evil children
- Because they can't find you a job

VEGANS — a good pseudo 'racial' insult

- 'Why don't you just fuck off back to Vega?'

VEGETARIANS — why you shouldn't become one

- *They* want you to
- People will think you're a loony or a New Age traveller and shun you
- You couldn't go to McDonald's with your mates any more
- They like sitting naked, cross-legged, worshipping the Pole Star in their spare time – or something like that
- Bacon butties
- Hitler was a vegetarian. Do you want him for a role model?
- Animals exist for us to eat: they wouldn't be bred otherwise, so, by eating meat, you're actually helping animals to continue
- What will you do at Christmas? Instead of the Christmas turkey, you'll have to face the Christmas nut roast . . .
- Have you ever tasted bean-curd soup?
- What you don't know won't hurt you

VEGETARIANS — good ways to annoy them

- Call them veggies
- Make endless jokes about them eating nothing but nut cutlets
- Tell them that they're not as committed as vegans
- Make them watch that film about the plane that crashes in a remote part of the Andes
- Tell them that their house was built on the site of an ancient Roman abattoir
- Torture a radish in front of them
- Torture *them* in front of a radish
- Hypnotise them into thinking they're Frank

221

Bruno then watch them devour a plate of rare steak. Record it on a camcorder for later playback, or send a copy to the local veggie club
- Cook them a sausage and tell them it's soya
- Kick them in the bollocks really hard with your leather shoes

VENEREAL DISEASE — politically incorrect songs to perform outside a VD clinic

- 'Great Balls of Fire' — Jerry Lee Lewis
- 'Blue Is the Colour' — Chelsea Football Club
- 'The Clapping Song' — The Belle Stars
- 'Every Day Hurts' — Sad Cafe
- 'Farewell My Summer Love' — Michael Jackson
- 'It Don't Come Easy' — Ringo Starr
- 'I Get Around' — The Beach Boys
- 'Easy Lover' — Philip Bailey and Phil Collins
- 'Love Hurts' — Jim Capaldi
- 'I've Got You Under My Skin' — Frank Sinatra
- 'It Started with a Kiss' — Hot Chocolate
- 'Pills and Soap' — Elvis Costello
- 'Purple People Eater' — Sheb Wooley
- 'Sexual Healing' — Marvin Gaye
- 'Among My Souvenirs' — Vince Hill
- 'Ain't Love a Bitch' — Rod Stewart

VICTORIAN VALUES — why Mrs Thatcher was right to want a return to them

- There's a tiny percentage of brothels in London today, compared to good old Victorian times, and back then you could enjoy a 'Thrupenny Upright' for three old pence. Imagine — you could shag yourself to death for a quid!

- There's nothing like putting your wife across your knee and beating her with your belt for resolving domestic difficulties
- We could give children useful things to do, like sweep chimneys, instead of wasting money on educating them
- Workhouses are an excellent solution to our increasingly ageing population
- You could pollute London all you wanted to, since the wind blows it all into the East End. (This may make life unpleasant in Docklands today, but then isn't it already?)
- You could get an erection just looking at a lady's ankle. (Today, most of us are so jaded we would be lucky if we could end up with one if we found ourselves in bed with the Barbi Twins)
- If you were well-to-do, people doffed their caps and called you 'Guv'nor'. Now they kick your head in and steal your briefcase
- Families of ten children would soon reverse the ageing population trend
- A back-street abortion was far more reliable than the morning-after pill (and more pleasant)
- Teenage joyriding in hansom cabs was a relatively rare event
- In those days, being British meant something. It still does today — you're a lazy, alcoholic, violent, uncouth lout

VIKING BERSERKERS — things which they considered politically incorrect

- Flower arranging
- Poetry
- Painting a still life
- Washing up
- Feminism
- Vol-au-vents
- Tobogganning
- Safe sex
- Tai Chi
- Washing under the arms

223

VIOLENCE — why it would spice up *The Archers*

EPISODE: 20,568 'Carnage In Ambridge'
<u>Date of Broadcast: 8.5.94</u>

(Theme music introduction)
SFX: (PUB SOUNDS; PEOPLE CHATTING, GLASSES CLINKING ETC.,)

JOE GRUNDY: If you ask me, Mr Archer, you should never have sold your farm to the Government for use as a toxic waste dumping ground. I've heard talk of some mighty strange happenings at Grey Gables, and them folks at Borchester seem pretty worried.

PHIL ARCHER: Come on, Joe, you're always listening to rumours.

MIKE TUCKER: Yes, I've also heard those ridiculous stories about a six-legged calf with the head of Benny Green being born, but you know what village folk are like.

SFX: (SCREAMS AND GLASSES BREAKING. CHAIRS AND TABLES ARE KNOCKED TO THE GROUND IN A MASS PANIC)

JOE GRUNDY: Oh my God! It's Grace Archer! She's returned as a charred and blackened hell-spawned flesh zombie!

GRACE ARCHER: (*Speech interspersed with the sound of heavily laboured breathing*) Yes, Joe . . . It's me . . . I've risen from the grave . . . I didn't want to die . . . Let me touch you . . .

PHIL ARCHER: (*Astonished*) Mother! How? . . . You're dead!

GRACE ARCHER: No, Phil . . . The radiation from the toxic waste . . . It's revived me . . . maggot-addled and pus-drenched!

JOE GRUNDY: (*Shouting*) Quick, everyone! Out the back door!

PHIL ARCHER: Is it really you mother? Let me touch you, if you're real . . .

224

MIKE TUCKER: (*Shouting*) No, Phil! Keep away! Keep away! Don't look at its eyes! Don't look at its eyes!

SFX: (SQUELCHING NOISE FOLLOWED BY BLOOD-CURDLING SCREAMS THAT SLOWLY DIE DOWN)

JOE GRUNDY: Mr Archer! Mr Archer! Oh my God!

MIKE TUCKER: Back, Joe! It's too late. Grace ripped his stomach open with her razor-sharp nails! Look how his intestines are slowly pulsating on the floor as she feeds on them ravenously!

JOE GRUNDY: I think I'm going to faint.

SFX: (POPPING SOUND FOLLOWED BY WET SPLATTERING NOISE)

MIKE TUCKER: Oh my God. Now Joe's brain's exploded! Ahhhhh! Ahhhh! My insides are churning and twisting like I'm being turned into something mucoid . . . It's the radiation . . . it has to be! . . . Ahhhhh! . . . Ahhhhh!

GRACE ARCHER: Michael . . . Do you really think you can escape me by transforming into a 6-foot bogie? Silly boy! I shall feast on you!!

SFX: (THE REMAINDER OF THE EPISODE CONSISTS OF SUCKING, SLURPING, BURPING AND SQUELCHING NOISES INTERSPERSED WITH VERY LOUD BLOOD-CURDLING SCREAMS IN STEREO)

Fade out to. . . . . (THEME MUSIC)

ANNOUNCER: Lots of animals were hurt in the making of this episode. Even though they didn't appear in it.

VIOLENCE — why there should be more of it on TV

- Unless you watch it, how will you become immune to it?
- It prepares you for life in the real world

225

- It redresses the balance with all those programmes with no violence whatsoever (like *Highway*)
- If you don't want to watch it you can always turn it off (or ask the kids to turn it off)
- How else are you going to attract big Hollywood talent like Jean Claude van Damme, Chuck Norris, Steven Segal or Dolph Lundgren?
- It captures the sizeable pre-teen audience
- Because paying your licence fee should entitle you to a say in the programmes they make
- Violence on radio just isn't the same
- The ratings will encourage companies who haven't advertised on TV before to start (e.g. Kalashnikov, Uzi, Smith & Wesson)
- After all, it's only art reflecting real life

VOLUNTARY SERVICE OVERSEAS — why you shouldn't ever apply for it

- You'll never get posted anywhere fun like New York or Paris
- Digging karsies in Malawi is no picnic
- Do they offer to come over to Britain and help solve our problems, like the national debt or the breakdown of law and order? Of course not. They couldn't give a monkey's about us
- You'll see things which will scar you for life and then you'll be sorry
- Malaria is not funny
- Neither is dysentery, especially when you have to share the only toilet with the entire Masai nation
- Dangerous animals, like snakes and tigers, live overseas
- Colonial guilt is passé
- The only thing on TV over there is their beloved leader giving some fascist speech and showing off his medals from reveille to shut-down. He

226

probably even does the weather, complete with propaganda
- It's the UN's job to sort these things out. Let them do it. Bloody authorities. Always wanting something for nothing

WAR POETS — why they were a waste of time

- Every minute spent writing was one minute they weren't killing the Hun
- Their poems didn't help the Allied war effort one little bit
- They should have been trying to win medals not literary prizes
- Instead of grappling with grammar they should have been grappling with the enemy
- They should have been splitting heads, not infinitives
- Only sissies write poetry
- Many of the war poems start off 'There was a young man in the Somme . . .' but since this rhymes very easily with 'bomb', it was seen as a major cop-out. (By comparison, very few poems were ever written about Ypres)
- Rhyming in World War I was easy when it came to the subject matter e.g. trench/stench, wire/fire, hun/gun, lead/dead, tri-plane/bi-plane
- Girls were more impressed by someone who'd lost an arm in Flanders than by someone who'd written an eight-line stanza

WELSH — what it really sounds like

- You're mad and gibbering
- A sing-along with Bill and Ben
- Gargling first thing in the morning
- German spoken backwards by Stanley Unwin on acid
- A feeble attempt at yodelling
- Not what it's spelt like
- A throwback to primitive times when language hadn't been properly thought through
- Helen Keller attempting to sing 'My Way'
- A protracted and particularly purging puke
- Someone urgently in need of the Heimlich Maneouvre

WELSH PUPPY FARMS — why they're a jolly good idea

- Participating in puppy farming gives hard-pressed local councillors a valuable extra source of income
- Pedigree forging by these establishments has become such a fine art that it is represented every year at the Eisteddfod as a genuine Welsh custom
- The Welsh are particularly good at inbreeding, so they can easily apply this to their dogs without revulsion
- Buying a golden retriever with 'rage syndrome' is a very good way of teaching children never to trust anything — no matter how lovely and furry and cuddly it looks
- A puppy with chronic hip displacement does a really funny, shuffly walk
- Welsh puppy farms help to keep local pet shops in business, by selling them sick 'pedigree' pups at 50 quid a throw which are then sold on to you at 200 quid plus. Not a bad little profit —

and since the pups are often dead within a year, the pet shops can be assured of repeat business

- They supply puppies for valuable cosmetic and medical research projects — like burns-trauma experiments, which could never be done on people
- They supply loathsome dealers who then advertise in your local newspaper that their dog has just had a litter of lovely pups — 'Only you can't see the mother, because she's resting/at kennels/gone to the country/feeling a bit tired'

WHALES — reasons why they should be harpooned

- Because an air pistol won't stop one
- If they weren't, hundreds of harpooners would have to be made redundant
- And the Norwegian steel industry would grind to a halt
- To prevent the wholesale slaughter of innocent plankton
- To avenge the tragic death of Captain Ahab
- They're a menace to international shipping and aircraft that have to ditch in the sea
- To prevent another near-tragedy like Pinocchio from ever happening again
- Their 'song' is bloody annoying when you're trying to get to sleep on a boat in the mid-Atlantic
- They're extremely dangerous (that's why they're called killer whales)
- Harpooning is far more practical than exploding a thermo-nuclear device down their spout hole

WHALES — why it's better not to adopt one

- It might sit on your lap for a cuddle
- Other children may tease it at school for being adopted

- A passing Japanese tourist might harpoon it and you'll be heartbroken
- Many Labour-controlled councils won't let you adopt one unless you yourself are of 'Aquatic Mammalian' extraction, to ensure it grows up in the right ethno-cultural environment
- When it grows to adolescence, it'll start to do the legendary 'song of the whales' and you won't be able to watch *Emmerdale Farm* in peace
- Sooner or later, it will want to know who its real mother and father are and you'll have to hire a big flatbed truck and drive it to the coast

WHEELCHAIRS — why we shouldn't feel sorry for people in them

- They can sit down wherever they go
- Some lucky buggers even get pushed everywhere
- Disabled access is not available in many theatres which — considering what's currently on — is a blessing for them
- They get to sit at the front at football matches
- They can't get on to public transport — which considerably reduces their chances of being mugged, raped, knifed or beaten up
- Disabled parking spaces are nearer the shops
- They can ride upstairs on those fun-looking lifts
- Employers don't like employing them — so they can lead a life of leisure
- Disabled access in most shopping malls is appalling, so they naturally end up with low credit-card bills at the end of the month
- Their arms are bloody powerful from all that wheeling, so if they feel you're patronising them they'll beat the living shit out of you

WHITBY — how it will be changed for the better by the greenhouse effect

- Thanks to its new, sub-tropical climate, Whitby will become renowned as 'The Home of the Idle Rich'
- New and exotic cocktails will be invented like the 'Humberside Skyliner' and the 'Durham Sloe Comfortable Screw', all made from the pineapples, bananas, oranges, peaches and mangoes grown locally
- Surfers will practise on the beaches for the forthcoming World Surfing Championship in Bridlington, just down the coast
- As ships full of rich tourists pull in, the Whitby locals (wearing flat caps, grass skirts and garlands) will row alongside to sell the passengers rock, Kiss-Me-Quick hats and other cheap, nasty souvenirs
- New species that inhabit the coastal waters will replace traditional fish dishes. Diners will enjoy marlin and chips, stingray in batter, barracuda fritters, flying fish cakes and swordfish in a basket
- Whitby will be very much geared to the sophisticated visitor with quality restaurants and nightclubs (many featuring 'topless lasses') lining the sea front
- Nevertheless, some of the area's traditional leisure pursuits will not be lost. Games of cribbage and dominoes and pub skittles will be played for big money in the casinos
- 'Putting a Jaguar Cub down Your Trousers' will replace the local sport that used to involve ferrets (before the jaguars ate them all)
- Tourists at Whitby will be able to travel on to see such wonders as the North York Rain Forest and the Great Hartlepool Reef

232

WIFE BEATING — some perfectly justifiable reasons

- It's her birthday and you forgot to give her something
- It's your birthday and it's your treat
- It's your wedding anniversary and you want to share the occasion
- It'll enable her to make new friends at a local support group
- It'll enable her to appear on *Kilroy* talking about her experiences
- It'll give her the chance to try out that new concealer stick
- You've finally found out which women's refuge she's been staying at

THE WIVES' CHARTER — things married women should be expected to do for their husbands

- Pervy and unnatural and quite sickening things he read about in one of his grubby mags
- Pretend you came too
- Wear stupid 'sexy' outfits when he can't get it up
- Be a font of sympathy when he's ill and try not to be an inconvenience and a nuisance to him when you're ill
- Spend 15 minutes a day at the sink trying to scrub away those stubborn skidmarks no washing powder ever boasts about removing (because they can't)
- Put up with his cretinous lechy friends who are always trying to get you into bed behind his back
- Smile patiently and understandingly when he goes on and on about some Page 3 girl and says you ought to have tits like that
- Pretend you feel like it whenever he does — and don't feel like it whenever he doesn't

- Understand that one bath a week is more than enough for most men

WINSTON CHURCHILL — why he set a bad example

- While thousands of men were being killed in action he stayed at home
- By being seen in public with his cigar, he encouraged people to take up smoking
- He was always bombing some city or another
- He went on jaunts to Yalta on taxpayers' money
- He invented the V-sign
- He gave warmongering speeches
- He never attempted to do anything about his weight problem
- He introduced rationing to the British people
- Unlike Hitler, Churchill wasn't a vegetarian
- His state funeral in 1965 brought traffic to a standstill

WOMEN — things they should never, never, never be entrusted with

- Secrets
- Your credit card
- How much you earn
- An account at Selfridges
- The remote control device for the television
- Recording something on the video for you while you're out
- The car
- An ex-Chippendale turned milkman

WOMEN — things they should say for the benefit of men

- Yes
- Yes, please . . .

- That was a wonderful dinner. Thank you. The least I can do is have sex with you now
- That was the best ten seconds' sex I've ever had . . .
- Yes, of course it's big . . .
- Don't worry, it happens to every man sometimes . . .
- Would you like me to wear the fishnets or the rubber catsuit tonight?
- How did you know it's always been my greatest ambition to appear in 'Readers' Wives'?
- I don't usually sleep with a man on a first date — but for you I'll make an exception
- Would you like your dinner now?

WOMEN — why they're really bad drivers

- They drive too slowly
- They stop suddenly when the traffic lights change to orange
- They're easily distracted by things like dogs darting across the road, children crossing between parked cars etc
- They often take their eyes off the road, such as when they look at traffic signs or their speedometer
- They always assume that no one's going to overtake on the inside
- They brake without warning when they approach zebra crossings
- They hold loads of traffic up by refusing to overtake on a bend
- And by insisting on keeping their distance from the car in front
- They suddenly swerve to avoid cyclists

THE WORKING CLASS — why they should be exterminated

- They do the Mexican Wave at public events
- They do the Birdie Dance at parties
- They love the Royal Family
- They eat kebabs and drop the greasy paper outside your house on the way back to their estate
- They buy their *objets d'art* from Woolworth's
- Jim Davidson is working class
- They say 'haitch' when they mean 'aitch'
- They move their lips when they read (which is infrequently)

WORKING HOURS — why Britain should have a longer working week than its EC colleagues

- If you're unhappy at home you'll be able to spend less time with your family
- And more time carrying on your affair in the stationery cupboard
- It will show other European countries that British employees are the hardest working in the EC (and they *will* need some convincing)
- If you get paid by the hour you'll be quids in
- If you're working longer hours you'll have less time to spend the money, enabling you to save more
- Because employees will be tired when they get home they'll be less likely to have sex and therefore the birth rate will stay low
- More employees will have heart attacks trying to put in all this extra time, leading to increased job opportunities for the young
- The extra time will be useful in order to correct mistakes that workers have made through having to work longer hours
- This will lead to increased overtime

opportunities, correcting the mistakes made in the extra time by workers trying to correct mistakes they've made earlier

- This will lead to working 22-hour days, seven days a week with companies eventually working flat out just to correct mistakes they made during overtime in the previous financial year

WORKING WOMEN — why they're not a good idea

- They can't lift five boxes of photocopying paper into the stationery cupboard on their own
- They burst into tears the moment anyone yells at them
- In the summer they wear short dresses and distract the men
- They're no use whatsoever to the company rugby team
- They get married then have two weeks off for a honeymoon when it's really busy
- They're always moaning about sexual harassment, just because someone touched them up behind the filing cabinets
- They always have days off to go on word-processing courses
- They go off and have babies, just when they're starting to be useful
- They're always away from their desks making cups of tea and coffee for people in the office
- None of them ever want to go on the firm's annual outing to the test series at Lords
- They get upset when anyone tells a really good dirty joke
- They don't go down the pub at lunchtime

WORKSHOPS — politically correct workshops the middle classes would just flock to . . .

- Improve yourself through Albanian peasant marquetry techniques
- Navel contemplation
- Yoga for world peace
- Third World yoghurt recipes
- How to grow Third World lesbian cacti
- Traditional dances of the emerging nations
- Mime as a vehicle for gender sub-text exploration
- Weave the Ecuadorian one-parent way

THE WORLD — how to be at one with it

- Jump out of an aeroplane at a great height with no parachute
- Bury yourself alive
- Have yourself cremated and your ashes scattered from the Space Shuttle
- Dig yourself a little hole in the back garden and have a crafty shag with the Earth when no one's looking
- Beat yourself up while sitting in a small box full of carbon-monoxide fumes
- Take your orders directly from Bill Clinton

WORLD MUSIC — why it's shite

- Adam Ant did it first (and better)
- It's difficult to take seriously any type of music that uses a nose flute
- It's uncool to play air-zither
- None of the artists use laser light shows, banks of speakers 40 feet high or revolving stages
- None of the groups smash up their instruments in a rocked-out frenzy — because they couldn't afford to replace them if they did

- If the group was any good a major cola manufacturer would sponsor it
- What's more impressive to your mates — the new CD from Guns 'n' Roses or one by Los Carraleros de Majagnal?
- Primeval rhythms and multiple drums went out with the Glitter Band
- You never see a teen world-music idol on the cover of *Just Seventeen*
- You can't sing the lyrics because most of the songs don't have any
- And those that do are in some obscure African or South American language consisting of 38 different clicking noises and a burp

MALCOLM X — why he was a prat

- X is a stupid surname
- Malcolm is a stupid first name
- Whenever he signed something, people thought he was illiterate and took the piss out of him
- People would often ask him to spell his surname, which sent him into a flying rage
- He would often get letters addressed to 'Malcolm Eggs'
- When he signed cards to men, they thought he was putting a kiss on the card, leading to several strained relationships
- Hotels wouldn't take his reservation seriously as they thought he was giving a joke name (at least that's what they said when he turned up and they saw he was black)
- To confuse the FBI, Malcolm X assumed a number of false identities including Malcolm Y, Malcolm T, Malcolm Q and Malcolm Z
- When this failed to work, he tried another set of false identities including Fred X, Barry X, Tony X and Billy X
- When educated people saw his name written

down, they sometimes erroneously referred to him as Malcolm 10. Others referred to him as Malcolm Cross, which usually got them a swift punch in the mouth

- Jokers would usually say 'Malcolm ex-what?' — which again was rewarded with a swift punch in the mouth. (The truth is 'Malcolm ex-burglar')
- His dad, a Baptist minister, was really hurt that he wouldn't keep the family name of Wankenstein

XENOPHOBIA — why it's justified

- If they aren't after your job then why are they here?
- Your partner *knows* they make better lovers
- The reason they speak differently is because they're talking about you and don't want you to know
- When they're consulting their maps in Trafalgar Square they're really plotting something terrible
- Don't their cameras look like the type that takes microfilm photographs of nationally important documents?
- Their backpacks are just the right size to conceal a radio transmitter and scrambling device
- Have you noticed that as soon as they arrive in this country they get rooms in hotels or guest houses?
- When you go to their country they make you drive on the wrong side of the road to try to get you killed
- When you watch subtitled films how do you know that what you see on the screen is what's being said?
- Germany

XR3i — how the ultimate in politically incorrect cars was created

- In the beginning God created Dagenham and it was without form and void, just like it is now
- On the first day God said 'Let there be Ford'. And there was Ford. And God saw that Ford was good and could turn out tasty cars
- On the second day God said 'Let there be a small family hatchback'. And God called the small family hatchback 'Ford Escort'. And it was mediocre
- On the third day God said 'Let there be a high-performance version of this tinny car'. And God called this high-performance Ford Escort the XR3. And God saw that it was well wicked
- On the fourth day God said 'Let there be a fuel-injected engine in this tasty car to make it even tastier'. And God called this even tastier car the 'XR3i'. And the Philistines beheld the XR3i in wonder
- On the fifth day God said 'Let there be all manner of optional extras so that the Philistines might impress the girlies of Sodom and Benfleet and know them'. And God called these optional extras 'a 200-watt sound system', 'sun roof', 'leather seats' and 'tinted glass'
- On the sixth day God said 'Let there be the ultimate accessory that will go forth and multiply throughout Essex and fill the Earth'. And God called the ultimate accessory the 'Furry Dice'. And it was bright pink. And the Philistines were well pleased and delivered unto the Lord the thumbs-up sign
- Thus, the XR3i was finished. And on the seventh day God rested because he'd done enough damage for one week

YEAR ZERO IN CAMBODIA — why the Khmer Rouge massacre was a good thing

- They shot all the intellectuals
- They shot all the spekky gits on the off-chance that they might be intellectuals
- They shot people who owned bicycles — which would be a sensible policy to improve safety on the road in Britain — and help to stamp out boring things like the Milk Race
- It proved once and for all how utterly useless the UN are, foreshadowing Yugoslavia
- It enabled David Puttnam to make a great film like *The Killing Fields*
- At least it was their own people they were committing genocide against, instead of another people — which is quite original thinking on their part. (Don't you wish the Welsh had thought of it first?)

YOGA — why kung fu is miles better

- No one has ever managed to relax an opponent to death

- The lotus position is no match for a flying kick to the head
- It's difficult to be menacing wearing a leotard
- Carl Douglas never recorded a brilliant record called 'Yoga Fighting'
- Or 'Dance the Yoga'
- With kung fu you don't need to waste time learning how to breathe — which every living person knows how to do anyway
- When it comes to philosophy, the only one you need to know is 'Get them before they get you'
- When you're being attacked by a mugger, knowing all about harmony with your fellow man won't be any help whatsoever

THE YOUTH OF TODAY — what we should do with them

- Sneak up behind them and hit them on the head with a large plank
- Tell them there's a 'Ultra Mega Rave Groove' happening on the Isle of Wight — then scuttle all the ferries in Cowes Harbour
- Call them up for National Service — then start a war with every other country on earth
- Take them gently aside and tell them what the 70s were really like . . .
- Rig every fucking Gameboy and NES in the entire world to explode
- Give them jobs — and let them learn how tough life really is
- Subject them to thorough DNA testing — to ensure they're not 'alien cuckoos' deposited on us like in *Children of the Damned*
- Check our doors and windows are locked whenever we spot one
- Make it a criminal offence to have zits and

blackheads — giving us an excuse to lock them up until they've matured
- Blame the parents (or parent)

ZEBRAS — why we should hate them

- You get eye-strain just looking at them
- They look like bad television interference
- They look like tasteless 1970s wallpaper
- If one ever went near a bar-code scanner, the whole electronic system would melt down
- Zebras are actually very fat, but the jammy bastards' stripes make them appear svelte on the veldt
- They don't taste particularly good, even with the most ingenious of sauces ...
- You can't ride them like proper horses
- They gave their name to the zebra crossing — that thing that crops up with an old blind man on it just as you've built up a really tasty head of speed ...

ZOOS — why we should keep them open

- The orang-utans are always good for a laugh
- It's preferable to pay a few quid to see a tiger in a zoo rather than £1,200 and have lots of

needles stuck in your bum so you can see one
in India
- There is no evidence to show that animals
  pacing up and down is a sign they are unhappy.
  The police and guardsmen at Buckingham Palace
  do this and no one says that they're disturbed
- It's better to be a zebra in a cage than elevenses
  for a pride of lions on the veldt
- If you close the zoos the animals will be kicked
  out on the streets and end up being run over
- You can throw the otters 5p pieces when the
  keepers aren't looking and the stupid bastards
  will try to eat them
- Hordes of South American pickpockets won't
  have anywhere to go
- They're the only places in Britain where you can
  go for a ride in a llama and trap
- There are already too few places in Britain where
  you can pay £1.20 for a cup of tea
- You can put your hand up your girlfriend's skirt
  in the reptile house and shout 'Look out, love,
  the mamba's loose!'

ZOOS — good ways of making them more interesting to visit

- Re-create Pearl Harbor using the chimps in
  radio-controlled model ships and dive bombers
- Dress the animals up in the national costumes
  of their countries so it's easy to tell where they
  come from
- Put up a big sign saying 'All You Kill, You Eat!'
- Surgically remove the hind quarters of two
  llamas, sew them back-to-back and re-create Dr
  Doolittle's 'Push Me Pull You'
- Make the lions and the zebras share a cage
- Hold a demonstration of seal culling every hour
  on the hour

- Show how, with a little gentle persuasion and a cattle prod, grizzly bears can be made to dance
- Turn part of the 'Children's Corner' into a realistic, working abattoir

ZOOS — insulting comments to make as you wander around the cages

Baboons — 'Don't fancy yours, mate'

Reticulated python — 'I got one of them in my trousers!'

Chimps — 'Oy, Darren — you're in here!'

Gorilla — 'Look out, lads — it's the missus!'

Blowfish — 'Look, lads, a *blow*fish. Huh, huh, huh!'

Rhinocerous — 'I didn't know the mother-in-law was visiting'

Hippopotamus — 'Oy, Pavarotti! Do us "Nessun Dorma"!'

Giraffe — 'Now that's what I call a deep throat, eh, lads?'

Sloth — 'Oy, Wayne — you're in here!'

Penguin — 'They're my favourite biscuits . . .'

Giant pandas — 'Go on my son, give her one! Get stuck in!'

Parrot — 'Go on, say it: my keeper is a wanker; my keeper is a wanker'

Elephant — 'Look, lads, Gazza's been transferred to the zoo!'

    OR: 'Go on, go on; why does an elephant have four feet?'

    OR: 'All right: What do you do if an elephant comes into your bedroom?'

Zoo keeper — 'Oy, where do you keep the Millwall supporters then?'

Toucan —   'Hold up, lads — it's Barbra Streisand!' (It would actually be funnier to say 'Hold up, lads — it's Jeremy Paxman' but, guaranteed, none

of your mates will ever have watched
Newsnight)

Horny Toad — 'Oy, Craig — you're in here!'

Cockatoo — 'Oy, Kev — your missus has had a
cockatoo, ain't she?'

Lion — 'Look, Dave — a big pussy! Bet you're
feeling homesick now!'

Warthog — 'Look, Steve — it's that bird you bin
seein'!'

Camel — 'These bleeders give me the hump!'

Giant porcupine — 'Look, lads! It's a load of
Chelsea fans. Wot a bunch of pricks!'

GLOSSARY

CUT THE CRAP — a guide to 'politically correct' 1990s speak!

It's about time we stopped using all these polite 1990s euphemisms and started calling a spade a spade once again, instead of a manually operated excavatory implement . . .

Academically challenged
  Thick
Academically challenged, longitudinally disadvantaged and double arboreally structured
  Thick as two short planks
Academically challenged by way of porcine excretive matter
  Thick as pigshit
Academically challenged person with perceived abnormal sexual requirements of senior years
  Silly old sod
Academically and posteriorally gifted
  Smart-arse
Anal intercourse
  People talking out of their proverbial backsides

while engaged in conversation. What's usually called, in polite circles, a 'dinner party'

Apollonian–Dionysian perplexity
Student dilemma whether to study or get pissed

Aptitudinally challenged
Social workers

Aqua-technic operatives
Bastard plumbers

Aurally confused and sartorially challenged
Anyone who likes rave music

Bovine, porcine and poultry-harvesting technician
Butcher

BSE
What the government will still be telling you is really Alzheimer's disease in another ten years

Care in the community
A clever government ploy to get us caring for sick and needy relatives 24 hours a day, instead of expensive NHS doctors and nurses

Care in the community, released into
Licensed to kill

Career motivated
Destined for a mid-life crisis

Cerebrally deficient and cranially tapered
Pinhead

Certaindeathophobia
Fear of working in an office with smokers

Challenging neighbourhood
Shitty dump

Chaos theory
Trendy way for science to shrug its shoulders and look puzzled

Chattering classes
Bastard yuppies for the 1990s

Circumferentially challenged
Fat

Community
  Crappy old council estates full of people who
  hate each other
Community policing
  Turning a blind eye to avoid a riot
Craftsperson
  Someone who makes hideous lopsided green
  pottery and then tries to sell it for 30 quid a
  throw at car-boot sales
Cranially inconvenienced
  Beheaded
Culturally disadvantaged
  Australian
Culturally and circumferentially challenged
  Clive James
Culturally impoverished
  Pleb
Cultural relativism
  It's OK for people to eat each other, as long as
  they're foreign. The same logic allows for people
  to be Nazis as long as they're German. Basically
  it's a way of making excuses for other people's
  crap customs

Deconstructionism
  A redundant method of breaking society down
  to see how it works — as it's already unravelling
  before our eyes
Deficient in terminological exactitudes
  Lying toerag
Designer
  A waste of money
Dexterously and fiscally rigid person of senior years
  Tight-fisted old git
Dolphin-friendly tuna
  Tuna-unfriendly food that's twice the price

Domiciliary disadvantaged
  People who are too stupid or lazy to keep their
  jobs and so get their houses repossessed
Dysfunctional family unit
  Those bastards from the local council estate who
  keep stealing the car stereo
Dysfunctional institution of limited jurisdiction
  The local council
Dyslexic
  Illiterate
Dystopian
  Life in the 1990s

Ecologically sound
  Doesn't work properly
Edibly disadvantaged
  Livestock
Emotionally challenged
  A person who is upset about something
Emotionally different
  Psychotic
Envelopment
  A less aggressive and more 1990s sounding term
  for sexual penetration
Environmentalist
  Someone who puts the 'mental' in
  environmental
Environmentally friendly
  Twice the price
Environmentally sound
  Twice the price — and it doesn't work
Ethnic cleansing
  A polite euphemism for 'genocide', which we all
  promised would never happen again, the use of
  which term enables the UN to turn a blind eye
Ethnically disadvantaged
  Anyone born in Belgium

European citizen
This could mean *absolutely anything* . . . or nothing

Everyday existence with female canine attributes
Life's a bitch . . .

Excretive proboscis merchant
Brown-noser

Existentially disadvantaged
Dead

Extra-marital illicit sexual congress with lactic provision supplier
Having it off with the milkman

Factually challenged
The *Sunday Sport*

Factually and academically challenged
Sunday Sport readers

Fascist
Anyone who doesn't agree with you

Financially challenged
Skint

Financially challenged and avariciously motivated
Lloyd's Name

Follically challenged
Bald

Follically and academically challenged, longitudinally disadvantaged and double arboreally structured
Skinhead

Fractals
Who cares?

Gastronomically challenged
Starving

Gender role reversal exploration
Secretly dressing up in your wife's clothes while she's out at the bingo

Gravitationally challenged
  Any person who finds themselves in the
  predicament of falling from a great height,
  probably face first

Homeless persons
  Workshy spongers
House husband
  Unemployed

Integrally inconvenienced
  Being blown into tiny pieces
Interest-reversal specialist
  Whoever taught you at school
Intestinal respiratory emission
  Fart

Japanophobia
  Fear that your children will never see a whale

Labelling theory
  The idea that, if you call a thieving little toerag
  a thieving little toerag, he'll become a thieving
  little toerag. (What useful concepts sociology has
  brought us over the years)
Latitudinally disadvantaged
  Northern
Latitudinally inconvenienced
  Having to visit the North for some reason
Lifestyle
  Middle class for what the rest of us call 'making
  ends meet'
Livestock remodelling practice
  Abattoir

Male domiciliary violence provider
  Wife batterer
**Male person of hygienically challenged and
  durationally disadvantaged status**
  Dirty old man

Mammarily disadvantaged
Flat-chested
Mammarily gifted
Chesty babe
Mime
Utter crap

New Age
A feeble excuse for Mike Oldfield to release
Tubular Bells II
New Age travellers
New Age parasites (also: dirty, scruffy, smelly,
hippy layabouts)
New man
Wimp
New woman
Old man
Nuclear family
A couple who are staying together 'for the sake
of the children' . . .

Ozone friendly
Won't come out of the can properly

Parenting
Increasingly neglected part-time occupation
Person of gender
A phrase applying to 99.9 per cent of the human
race
Person of phallically cranial disposition
A dickhead
Person of race
A totally useless phrase, as *everyone* is a person
of race; usually used only by middle-ranking
police officers sat before a promotions board
Person of substance
Once a polite way of referring to a rich git;

nowadays used to describe someone who you wouldn't want to share a fragile-looking lift with

Personal hygiene deficiency
BO

Phallically challenged
Female

Politically aware
Being able to name the Shadow Secretary for Transport

Politically correct
Bollocks

Positive thinking
Pretending that the world isn't like it is

Positively challenged
Tall young white heterosexual middle-class male in perfect health

Private Health Care
An excuse to run down the NHS

Pro-Lifer
Someone who tries to tell someone else what to do, usually in the name of Jesus. Believes in the sanctity of life above all else, and then goes home and enjoys a big steak dinner

Property procurement operative
Thief

Psychobabble
What you and I would call 'talking crap'

Psychologically challenged
Someone who wanders around in a drool-stained T-shirt thinking they're receiving secret instructions from Nanette Newman or Sooty

Quality time
The province of the idle rich

Racist!
Useful 'politically correct' term of abuse for anyone you disagree with, ranging from the

British National Party to the milkman whose
bill you're querying

Recidivist
Someone they should never have let out of jail
in the first place

Recycled
More expensive than the original

Reptilianly talented
Anyone in the legal profession

Resignationally imminent
Just about any government minister you can
name

Right-on
Term of abuse for someone who's even more
Politically Correct than you

**Sartorially challenged male person of transitory
urban existence**
Tramp

Self-defence
The most serious crime you can currently
commit

Self-realisation
Making lots of money and never having to do
another stroke of work again

Senior citizen
A potentially misleading term for the lowest
rank in the British social order

Sexist
Sexist

Significant other
Important people in your child's development,
e.g. the one who teaches them the F word or
gives them their first cigarette

Socially aware
Spending a quid in the local Oxfam shop every
fortnight

Socially dexterous
  Insincere
Socially disadvantaged
  Spotty geek
Socially inconvenienced
  Having to be nice to someone you hate
Soirée
  (See under 'Anal Intercourse')
Soliciting non-earned gratuities
  Begging
Sunophobia
  Middle-class fear of the *Sun*'s circulation figures

Talentially challenged
  Rolf Harris
Territorial transgression specialist
  Burglar
Territorial transgression specialists with special voiding requirements
  Burglars who piss up your wall and shit in your knicker drawer
Truth-reversal executive
  Estate agent

Unwaged
  Piss poor
User friendly
  Something that, nine times out of ten, is just the opposite

Vertically challenged
  Short-arsed
Vertically, circumferentially and talentially challenged
  Neil Sedaka
Virtually fat free
  Still very high in calories

Visually inconvenienced
Blind
Vocally–anally interfaced
Talking out of your arse

Work-deference specialist
Student
Workshop
Any activity at which lots of middle-class liberal gits get together and ponce around to no real effect

Zoomorphically Disadvantaged
Pig ugly

FURTHER READING

If you have enjoyed this book you might wish to read more about Political Incorrectness.

The following list of titles serves as a guide to some of the most influential works on the subject.

Mein Kampf: Hitler, A.

It Wasn't Me, It Was the Others: Mengele, J.

No It Was Him. I saw Him Do It: Bormann, M.

And Me!: Hess, R.

Conservative Party Manifestos 1979–92: Conservative Central Office

Adolf and Me: Mussolini, B.

Love Me, Love My Land: Terreblanche, E.

Everything You Ever Wanted to Know About Subjugating Minorities But Were Too Afraid to Ask: Serbian League of Genocidal Maniacs, 1992

Let's Go Vivisection!: Shampoo Manufacturers Guild, 1988 (reprinted 17 times)

Which Dangerous Dog?: Consumers' Association Special, 1990

Flag Burning For Beginners: Iraqi Student Union Publications, 1991

Book Burning For Beginners: Iraqi Student Union Publications, 1991 (634th reprint)

Exploiting the Planet for Fun and Profit — An Economic History of America: Dodds, C. M.

Build Your Own Chemical Weapon Plant in Just Four Days!: The Salaam Press, 1992

The Observer Book Of Repression: 5th edition, 1991

Bluff Your Way in Mindless Racism: Popular Press, 1993

I Spy Immigrants: HMSO, 1958

Every Boy's Book of Abattoirs: Meat Traders' Federation, 1961

ATTENTION ALL BABES!

Do you like books?

Do you wear a bikini?

Do you want to keep abreast of all the latest news and gossip about Mike Lepine and Mark Leigh?

Do you go?

If the answer to all the above is 'YES' (especially the last one) then you should join the MIKE & MARK FAN CLUB

What's more — it's absolutely free!

Some of the most commonly asked questions about the MIKE & MARK FAN CLUB:

What's in it for me?
- The chance to get news of Mike & Mark's writing exploits *before* they hit the TV screen or bookstalls
- A colour photo of Mike & Mark to treasure forever
- Your very own membership card
- A lock of their hair (while stocks last)
- A welcome letter *personally signed*
- The chance to win autographed copies of future books
- And much, much more
- And much, much, much more

Sounds good so far but what does it cost to join?
Nothing.

Pardon?
Nothing. That's right — no money at all. All you have to do is send a photo of yourself in a bikini. It's as simple as that!

Sounds too good to be true! I'm all for it! What do I do now?

Complete the form and stick it on the back of your photo and send it to the publishers at the address below with an SAE. (Remember, an SAE is vital considering the royalties these boys are on.)

*

Please send your photo and SAE to:

THE MIKE LEPINE & MARK LEIGH FAN CLUB
c/o VIRGIN PUBLISHING
332 LADBROKE GROVE
LONDON W10 5AH

Dear Mike and Mark: I'm hot for it (your fan club, that is).

Name ....

Age ....

Vital statistics ....

Address ....

.... Postcode ....

Do you have a boyfriend who is a member of any of the following organisations? Royal Marines (   ) SAS (   ) World Wrestling Federation (   ) Her Majesty's Prisons (   ) The Triads (   )

Small print:
Due to legal reasons membership is restricted to babes aged between 16–35
P.S. The bit on the inside front cover about Mark being married is a misprint